Counselor Self Care

Reflections on Interpersonal Wellness

Bette Katsekas

"Counselor Self Care," by Bette Katsekas. ISBN 978-1-62137-060-4.

Published 2012 by Virtualbookworm.com Publishing Inc., P.O. Box 9949, College Station, TX 77842, US. ©2012, Bette Katsekas. All rights reserved. No part of this publication may be reproduced, stored in a retrieval system, or transmitted in any form or by any means, electronic, mechanical, recording or otherwise, without the prior written permission of Bette Katsekas.

Manufactured in the United States of America.

Introduction: The Essence of the Energy of Helping

Not too long ago, I discovered in my reflections that there were some unexpected connections between the worlds of psychotherapy, science and mathematics. Basic principles that gave these diverse fields their power and energy appeared to all be related somehow. For example, in both therapy and science, attention impacts reality. In the counseling field, we certainly recognize the everlasting power of attentive listening; in physics, we see from the infamous "double slit experiment," where the mere act of observation alters the results of an experiment; how the power of observation alters the intricate relationship to reality itself. Quantum science especially has blurred these lines of where the mind ends and external "reality" begins.

The second area of unexpected connections that I reflected upon was in the area of relationships, or in a physical sense, relatedness. In counseling, as in life, we know "it is all about" relationships. Relationship issues seem to be an area of concern that brings many people to the counseling process. The counseling relationship or therapeutic alliance is essential in order for therapy to work at all. In science, Einstein taught us that everything exists in relation to everything else. Perhaps relatedness or process is the fundamental unit of our universe and not a separate "thing" in and of itself.

Thirdly is the area of thought. Our universe tends to be very thought sensitive and that cognition appears frequently if not always, to precede manifestation. This is

1

true in mathematics. For example there is no such thing in actual realty as a perfect circle, yet this pure idea of a circle has fed the essence of our civilization. "Pi" does not precisely exist yet we use this idea every day in many situations. In counseling, we have goals, visualizations, miracle questions, picture albums and so on that lead to actual behaviors. This is most likely true in sports psychology.

And finally, there is the essence of meaning (or our context) and that we are more than we seem. Reality is more than what appears. We live in a multidimensional and complex world, most of which we can't see. Our physical lives are likely to only be one very small piece of the picture, especially if we live in numerous higher dimensions as is theorized by many scientists.

These four areas summarized above, individually and together form a kind of quantum 4 step, areas of "quantum crossovers," or sustainable energy that we could use for wellness every day: to learn to listen better (with love, and unconditional positive regard); to relate effectively , to ourselves, others and our context; to think clearly and responsibly, and likely this will manifest; and finally to connect, to consciously be aware that we are embedded in layers of complexity and meaning that are far beyond our limited space-time thought processes and imaginations.

Listen, relate, think and transcend.

This mantra is a condensed representation of the spirit behind many of the reflections that follow. I hope you find them helpful, emotionally sustaining, and self-renewing as I have over the years. As counselors, teachers, and parents, or when in any other type of helping role, we often find ourselves in this world, in relation, exchanging powerful energy. I suspect that deep down we all possess a deep desire to heal and promote an interpersonal atmosphere of wellness. It is in this spirit that these daily thoughts are offered.

January 1

The concepts of love, happiness and interpersonal wellness are important constructs to pay attention to, identify and explore throughout our lives. There is no question that our mental health diagnostic system, that is, assigning a name to a problem, helps us to establish goals for a better life. But we need to pay less attention to pathology at the expense of further definition and discussion of healing concepts such as hope, optimism, happiness or what is referred to in this book as interpersonal wellness. This is an area counselors are expert at developing.

Most of us cannot deny the importance of seeking further happiness. But this cannot be an open-ended search without a basic set of ideas from which to work. These thoughts and meditations presented in this book might help in some small way in developing a more positive state of emotional health. Love, hope and happiness can be explored from the point of view of interpersonal wellness, an important dimension often overlooked in our social culture of work, technology and task orientation.

January 2

At the end of our lives, we rarely wish we had accumulated more things. When someone is dying, there are few documented examples of people who wish that during their lives they had collected more things. But very often, we wish that we had spent more time working on improving our relationships with others and expressing our love more clearly and directly. We sense that interpersonal wellness is essential to our overall well-being and a happy life.

By identifying, exploring and learning to express certain specific behaviors in explicit ways we can help ourselves have a more loving quality of life. These behaviors involve the language of positive regard, respect and noticing the strengths and positive qualities of others.

January 3

The concept of interpersonal wellness may help to promote a higher level of interpersonal success. Daily thoughts and meditations related to important relationships may help further advance the dialogue of interpersonal peace, happiness and mindfulness in our world.

Our interpersonal relationships occupy a sacred space. Important relationships teach us lessons about life. At times these lessons are painful, at other times, the learning is joyful. If we remain open to this continuum of learning, life is full of small miracles every day.

January 4

It is worth the time to develop a greater appreciation for what love is and recognize that it has many forms. There are numerous ways to know love in the moment. Each day we learn through carefully observing and identifying ways to express love to others.

The love focused life is a rewarding one. Often our major tests and lessons occur in the context of pain, adversity or ongoing stress. The focus on a more loving perspective is powerfully healing especially when times are tough.

January 5

Positive thoughts and natural abilities emerge when distractions and negativity are removed. Removing obstacles in love's way allows more room for positive connections. Unconditional positive regard is a natural resource that can nurture well-being both for the listener and the speaker.

Removal of negativity from our emotional daily connections can elicit active forgiving and letting go of the ego's controlling plans for others. Practice of this simple behavior of focusing the best in others and yourself leads to trusting more in the natural loving energy forces of the universe.

January 6

Interpersonal wellness begins with a positive cognitive focus. By focusing on the energy of love and thinking in a more focused and lovingly principled way, interpersonal dynamics dramatically change.

Awareness and implementation of this focus has a powerful impact, and unleashes a potent force in our day-to-day lives. It is amazing how we daily go about our work, busily focusing on the things around us rather than the forces of life's deepest blessings, our relationships with others.

January 7

Interpersonal wellness and relational health are based on the concept of loving detachment, warmth, caring without control, and genuine loving of others, without unrealistic expectations or false adoration.

True caring and authenticity are the greatest gifts we can give to one another. In the face of life's challenges, these gifts are worth more than any amount of money or material thing. The flow of energy between us is what vitalizes us and gives a healthy foundation of being. Relationships are the vehicles by which we grow and change in the interpersonal giving of ourselves to one another.

January 8

In order to maintain interpersonal wellness one way is to think of being-in-the-world as a *total* person--physically, mentally, spiritually, and emotionally.

Each of us has an immense capacity for loving and connecting with others. There is the potential for more loving interpersonal energy in this world than we realize. As you deeply listen and validate the others in your life, watch this potential energy force of love release around you. It does not require much energy from one another to unlock these loving forces and the potential within us.

January 9

Creating relational awareness on a daily basis translates into giving up a perspective of self-orientation and a prioritizing of inner thoughts. Creating this awareness allows us to follow a program with a more total integration of our loving self in relation to others.

Spiritual or emotional growth will not progress with an ego orientation. Living with an awareness of interpersonal wellness offers us more energy, freer flow of caring between people, and a healthier climate overall.

January 10

Learning to love at the deepest levels means visualizing one's self as a healthy and loving being, living on a kind, connected earth, with sound interpersonal ethics guiding all of our interpersonal relationships.

The practice of ethical behavior toward one another requires thinking of ethics not as a static set of cognitive principles but as mindful behaviors in relation to others. In other words, finely tuned intellectual ideas are nothing without genuine caring and offering one's best to others.

January 11

To fully comprehend interpersonal wellness is to consistently recognize potential loving connections that exist in unexpected places every day. Expressions of love should never be reserved solely for special occasions such as holidays, church services, hospital visits, or funerals. Interpersonal wellness involves developing a positive, loving and nonjudgmental set of feelings, in other words, an around-the-clock feeling of spirituality in relation.

It means growing at the deepest levels and generating good will toward others within one's inner spiritual levels. Interpersonal wellness is the foundation of happiness. Creating healthy and healing feelings with an ever-present focus on love is central to a counselor's work.

January 12

Authentically connecting with others is one of the most gratifying, energizing, and hopeful experiences in the world. This fact is unrealized and it is an untapped energy source for many of our relationships. Authentic or real connections with one another are often synergistic and build further connections of phenomenal potential and interactive power in life.

Identification of daily gratitude in relation to others will assist this potential and power to increase. These are the crucial steps- to recognize, identify and express authentic loving energy. It is all around us.

January 13

Useless defenses, especially those involving control over others use up our interpersonal energy to no benefit and often cause additional stress. Our deeper self needs more room to positively shift and advance itself to more healing levels. By peeling away and removing our useless defenses and moving toward our interpersonally sacred connection with life, we leave more room for our deeper and more loving essence to emerge. Doors open as interpersonal wellness moves us toward a happier, healthier and full life maximizing our potential on all levels of being.

January 14

To focus on one's self and articulate positive goals in life is an admirable and desired state of being. Yet to do so without yielding to a state of self-centeredness and narcissism is even more admirable. Working on this involves a critical balancing of self-care and a concern and love for others. One without the other does not work well. It is important to heal our past and painful relationships in life.

Our existence involves our being with others. Otherwise, each soul would find itself alone, each in separate places, scattered about the globe. In our relationships, love is the most important element there is.

January 15

As human beings we would do well to acknowledge that each and every other human being matters deeply and significantly within all of our relationships. Too many boundaries between us easily lead to rigid walls just as too few boundaries often lead to a merging of the self with others. A controlled venting of feelings with a subsequent focusing on one's self may feel good in the short term, but this style of communicating does not lead to a more enhanced relationship with others. There are many interpersonal balances to attend to in life. Mindful daily work to obtain our optimal relational health is as crucial to our overall heath as physical exercise.

January 16

Learning an awareness of feelings (along with an expression of feelings) helps to create a life that is overall more balanced. An out of focus life can result in a lack of an accurate cognitive awareness of others, even losing contact with our own authentic individuality. The reality is that what we share here, on this planet, along with its resources, energy and interconnection with other people is rooted deeply within our collective psyche. Our feelings are the most helpful guides in doing our work here.

January 17

Relationships are essential to life. Each human being is born into a group, family, and community, for better or worse for that individual. We usually do the best we can with what we have been given. People are social creatures by nature, and ultimately our purpose must have something to do with the fact that there are many of us here together. The purpose of life should not be the process of endlessly focusing upon the singular self. Interactions with others are our primary spiritual tools, and they provide a learning framework for life's crucial spiritual lessons.

January 18

All that is said or done, especially in relation to others, during each moment of every day of life, matters tremendously in the overall scheme of things. Everything counts spiritually. Everything matters in relation to other people.

There is available guidance within our midst from many sources. There has been considerable emphasis, especially in recent years, on living in community with others and the fact that our earth is indeed a global village. This has been underscored by the arrival of online, easily available worldwide communication. The Internet is a powerful metaphor for human connection. The message of connection, a spiritual message, comes to us each day, from many different sources and perspectives.

January 19

What could possibly be of significance in our simple day-to-day interactions with others or what is often termed the so-called "small things" of life? Not enough can be said of love's role in these daily events along with respect, kindness, and peacefulness. In our daily lives, we encounter situations at work, within our families, or in those quick, seemingly inconsequential impersonal encounters with others, that offer to us the opportunity for a greater level of awareness of interpersonal mindfulness. Often, when there is no interpersonal mindfulness there is much stress.

Value and respect the I-thou connection, that special place of interpersonal energy that naturally exists between us. This is the interactive realm, the rich realm of the in-between.

January 20

Every relationship or interaction is sacred in some way. The concept of relational sanctity needs to be further identified, developed, and expressed through our conscious practice of interpersonal mindfulness. Interpersonal wellness can flourish so easily if we allow it. And one of the major, pleasant outcomes will be a deeper and more satisfying, connective level of happiness in daily life.

January 21

How spiritual is it to exchange small talk for as little as two minutes on any given day? For even a few moments, there exists an essence of the reality of human connection between two people. While it may not be the presence of high-level immediacy or intensively dramatic, there is still the shared-in-the-moment kind of experience, a relational exchange. In every relational exchange, there is the substance of the higher purpose of life. Relational exchanges are the essential spiritual and educational dynamics of our conscious human lives. Every interaction we have, or to put it another way, every element of this relational medium, involves our thoughts, feelings, perceptions, reactions, intuitions, and projections, at any given and unique time, with another person or persons.

January 22

Every human interaction requires a focus on loving sanctity. Building block by building block, no matter how short the interpersonal exchange may be and no matter where or how it takes place, it will lead us toward our higher selves if we allow it. Releasing the enormous hidden potential that is possible will lead us to a more peaceful and nurturing reality in our lives. Whoever or whatever one believes to be the driving force of this universe or the loving primary forces of creation interpersonal exchange is a part of it. It is clear that humanity has not fully reached its fully developed life force of nurturing its divine development. In other words, humanity has not taken enough responsibility to develop its more loving side.

January 23

Emotions shared with others in relation are meant to be enjoyed and enable closer feelings to develop between people. There is a need to stop running and defending from this reality, through our daily distractions, such as overwork or denial. Enjoying one another often leads to enhanced positive energy, an exchange that can be experienced as a healing event.

January 24

Interpersonal wellness (our theme), and its related concepts of interpersonal mindfulness (the practiced behaviors) and connective happiness (our overall, guiding construct that results) all deal with living with a sense of spirituality in relation. These daily readings relate to these elements as realistic components of our spiritual development. Spiritual development is just as important to our human development as our physical or mental development.

January 25

The notion of interpersonal wellness has been partly influenced by our changing paradigms of science. A deeper dialogue and appreciation concerning the essence of relationships (in other words that relationships are more than what they appear) and other mysteries of life characterize the reality that relating to one another is more than it seems. This reality is happening in ever-increasing ways in our world. We all need to develop a lucid sense of the practice of loving and caring more deeply about one another as we go about our daily business.

January 26

The many uses and interactions of relational health, (that is, living within a context of mindfulness and creating positive and loving energy with others) give us a sense of the available positive power and energy that exists not only between people but within our species as a whole. It is evident that untapped power exists between human beings, and between humans and other species, such as humans and their pets. Love is a moving and powerful force.

January 27

There is a relationship between the purity of the human spirit and the deeper reverential behaviors and connections that exist between human beings on a feeling level in everyday life. The mindful awareness of this kind of connection encourages and focuses upon a more loving human condition.

We know more and feel more about one another than we consciously realize or appreciate. There is more potential in connections with others than we know. We are all wiser than we know.

January 28

Emotional pain, an important and obviously intended part of life, can be of help in giving us a more in-depth and meaningful, spiritual understanding of what it means to live in a decent and loving context. As our unconscious awareness turns more into a conscious awareness of our capacity for love, there will be a healthy amount of energy unleashed. Feelings are our guides, even emotional pain, and dreams of a loving planet become more commonplace with a newly balanced emotional reality.

January 29

The increased focus on a collective and loving quality of humanity could change the energy of our interpersonal universe. This kind of focus, on interpersonal mindfulness, could lead us into a new awakening and clear out unnecessary negativity and spiritual sludge. This interpersonal morass, which usually consists of unwarranted fears, or collective denials of our more loving selves, often can lead to abuse or the indulgence of food, alcohol, work, drugs. It holds our energy back, keeps love repressed. Emotional sludge blocks the path of greater loving energy and positive regard toward one another.

January 30

Every bit of positive energy that develops within the self adds to an overall transformation of spirit. Keeping a positive focus is essential. These daily readings go over some ideas for this process. By rising above many situations of life, such as old resentments, jealousies and false pride, all counterproductive to interpersonal growth, we move more easily toward interpersonal wellness.

January 31

The celebration and appreciation of interpersonal wellness increases overall happiness once an initial awareness is established and regularly nurtured. Any daily reading concerning an aspect of interpersonal wellness can be helpful in this process of learning. We can immediately and effectively see how our interpersonal pain is transformed when framed within a context of the inherently loving human spirit.

February 1

What is carried within the unconscious mind ultimately gets played out in conscious life. There is a vast amount of untapped energy and mystery within both the conscious and the unconscious mind. The essence of our humanity lies in the energy within and between us. Each mind perceives and affects others. We each present powerful energy to the world.

February 2

Loving energy connects our sense of inner peace and compassion within ourselves and between others. By observing and recognizing this loving energy field, we communicate something deeply toward others. In gravitating toward or worshipping the great and compassionate spiritual leaders of our world, such as Jesus, Buddha, Gandhi, Mother Teresa, and others, we demonstrate this every day. Loving energy speaks to the infinite, inherent power and spiritual ability within each of us, as well as with our most charismatic spiritual leaders.

February 3

Think for a moment of all of the human characteristics and physical presences that are in your daily life and of your innermost and deeper loving self. For example, what do you see when you watch an adult holding a baby, a person walking a dog, or two friends hugging? How do you feel? In reflecting on these kinds of interactions, feel their energy. They form the backbone of our authentic loving essence. This innermost sense of attachment and love is one of the most powerful forces that exist in our universe. Such a force holds the elements of the rest of our lives together.

February 4

Counseling and therapy were created to deal with inter psychic (between people) or intra psychic (within a person) elements. Therapy work is typically placed within a framework of goals, expectations and boundaries in order to be ethically practiced. Yet, the deeper work of healing the inner self is often a slow and painful process in order to be effective and long lasting. There are parts of this work, such as developing happiness, joy or love that have not received adequate or enough attention.

Consistent, gentle, daily practice with interpersonal wellness is a beginning, and could radically boost not only innermost levels of love and inner healing, but also help to connect our collective psychological spirit.

February 5

There is no substitute for work that must be done for self-improvement, such as reducing stress, losing weight, quitting smoking and so on, but interpersonal mindfulness is an essential context. The foundations of interpersonal wellness add to the healing process of the interpersonal and intra personal webs that connect each of us in our daily lives.

February 6

An essential principle of personal growth is that improvement in one area often improves another area. A more loving focus within one's self may begin to positively impact other areas of life. The process of interpersonal wellness affects one's inner self. The human psyche presents itself both within an individual and to our social and family groups, in a more transpersonal, larger, cultural context.

February 7

Feelings of love connect all humans. We seek them out, regardless of our culture or heritage. Each human being recognizes fear, belonging, intimacy and connection with others. Self-improvement, when emphasized simply for the purpose of the self, loses other energy forces available to it such as the fields of connective, loving energy that unites all of us.

February 8

What is really important to you in this life? When, where, and how, is the presence of loving energy from others in your life? There is so much more to any one of us than it may at first seem. There is a loving and powerful world of feelings that has barely been tapped into, especially in relation to one another.

February 9

Our innermost thoughts, feelings, ideas, prayers, creativity, or beliefs in God, a higher power or energy source, our physical senses, intuitions, and more, all form an impressive array of different aspects of our energy field and the potentiality of our divine human source. There is an outer self that each of us presents to the external world, one that consists of behaviors, actions, interactions, levels of productivity, as well as our outward physical appearance. Aspects of the inner self and outer self both represent a sacred interpersonal being.

These two aspects of the self, the inner and outer, cannot be separated as each set of energies is strongly connected to and influenced by the other.

February 10

One's rich inner reality affects the outside world and vice versa. Interpersonal mindfulness works with this truth. That is, the more love becomes a reality and energy is nurtured within the inner world; the more it connects with and affects the outer world, the world of our daily, interpersonal life.

By the same token, the more love that is expressed in all of its varied forms, the richer and more loving our inner life becomes.

February 11

More than something linear or causal, love is a connecting principle that is very powerful. It is synergistic energy, and the sum of its parts is greater than what one would normally anticipate. Its growth-inducing qualities are contagious, especially if regularly practiced. Connective happiness is more easily identified, explored, and expressed within one's life. The more individuals are willing to begin to practice a kinder and more loving style, the more likely we are to move toward a "critical mass" of change, progressively toward a more compassionate and spiritual state, perhaps even a major jump in our emotional evolution.

February 12

What is your deepest understood sense of how pure energy manifests? It may be through people, places, things, and ideas, anything that gives you a positive and loving gracious quality to your life.

By focusing in on, and then trying to sense the connection or flow between your awareness and your conscious mind, the pure energy in your daily living begins to surface more comfortably. The dynamics of interpersonal wellness occur within connecting spaces, the spaces in between you and others. It is in these "connecting spaces" that the life forces of energy exist. Simply by thinking of them more we can experience this.

Meditate about the various elements in the different aspects of your life during each day or before going to sleep at night and keep the energy going. By intentionally applying this greater focus, unnecessary destructive dynamics should begin to dissolve and make way for a more interpersonally focused way of life.

February 13

Focusing on old negative energies (between or within others), is the opposite principle of interpersonal wellness. It tends to decrease our energy and its positive flow. There is no advantage to this process.

Feelings and spiritual expressions are deeply connected, and this positive energy can be jump started, or begun, in any area of your life, emotional, physical, mental or spiritual.

The work of the mind is most powerful when it is given a positive foundation from which to do the work. This positive focus, this work on generating love's potential will hopefully help you more with this overall process.

February 14

The cultivation of interpersonal wellness involves a recognition that while love is the most powerful positive energy force there is it is also the most underutilized. More work can be done in the area of love's recognition, identification and creative expression. There are more and varied ways to tap into loving power. The spirit of this book and the ideas within it are only one option, one choice, among many different possibilities of working toward this change.

February 15

More practice is needed in understanding wellness from an interpersonal perspective. Most people, for example, in nearing the end of their lives, rarely lament on the lack of enough money, or a more successful job, a bigger car or house. But there is often a deep regret of not having shared enough, of not having generated enough good will, or affectionate interpersonal energy. Deep down we know that a more fully loving demeanor and essence matter most in this life. Practicing this work of daily compassion brings with it a divinely inspired sense of empowerment.

February 16

To deeply love others does not mean enabling or rescuing others from their true selves, or to live in denial and run away from the natural and human pains of life. It means more fully being a pure soul with a more loving state of mind. This process is facilitated by the practice of focusing on the power of positive and loving thinking. Appreciating that while each of us may be different from one another, there is a strong connection through a loving web of spiritual dynamism that connects us all. Practicing life in a modality of deep kindness allows for integration of the emotional nature of life. Life in general is meant to be a celebration of the thoughtful spirit.

February 17

Our rich spiritual roots are everywhere. Access to these roots is easier than it might at first seem. Our thoughts and minds are powerful and they are able to access this energy. Every human being is born with a divine sense of love. This can be observed in the energy that surrounds babies or young children prior to the fuller development of their more consciously socialized, or rational minds, and prior to their having learned how to defend against this natural, loving spontaneity. It is a sad loss. Love and humor are deeply felt instincts that can be easily re-recognized and re-nurtured. As our aging process occurs and we mature into elders, there is a remarkable return back to the desire to access these natural energies again. This is another potent demonstration of what our natural essence will do without its emotional clutter.

February 18

At the very end and beginning of life humans are most aware of an inherent interpersonal wellness. It is as if something needs to be left or lost during the middle portion of our lives in order to appreciate love more. There is a vast and loving storage space of energy that is left untapped throughout most of life. This could be garnered more during the bulk of human life. In other words, it could be developed more during the time of our life span. This would assure a more solid connection with our divine state while living in our physical state. There is no longer a need to be estranged from this deep self. There is no need to live in an alienated, preoccupied, stressed out, or scared state. We all have a strong need to connect more authentically with one another.

February 19

There is a wealth of positive thinking literature and many books and workbooks that deal with working on the expression and appreciation of love. There is much to read, listen to, work on, and nurture when it comes to the knowledge and greater expansion of love's role. Hopefully, these readings of interpersonal mindfulness will add to these works and help elicit more activity in this direction as one more method in fostering our return to this more natural state of loving mindfulness.

February 20

Acts of kind behavior, inner healing thoughts, or deep prayers will increase our loving energy. It is an exciting prospect on many levels, individual, group, or cultural.

The journey of our loving actualization has a beginning, but in reality, no end. The higher and more loving self has infinite potential to generate compassionate expressions in our daily lives.

February 21

The initiation of loving feelings, breeding a sense of positive good will and the realization that no one is any better or worse than anyone else, are all necessary threads to connecting these readings together. Any one individual's loving journey cannot be compared with another's. Interpersonal wellness is unique to each and every individual's specific personality. By using these readings and meditations, a deeper recognition of the daily miracles in life and in nature will hopefully become stronger with each passing day.

February 22

Think of ten things that make you a uniquely divine person and then write them down. This kind of appreciation of your own uniqueness can begin to work unconsciously.

Your more loving nature is always with you. This can be a powerful recognition, to cherish your own uniqueness and then to allow yourself to relish it. The similar remarkable qualities of others and what you have together in any kind of a relationship is sacred space. Notice these connections in your life. They are the beginning and the end, the spiritual foundations of the divine interpersonal life.

February 23

Life is much more than it seems. The reflections of transcendent goodness are evident in many of our relationships. The power of relational sanctity is evident with the mindful practices of kindness. It is all a part of our natural state to feel the process of love and the teaching powers of hurt, pain and rejection as well. Because of our inner, wounded feelings, we may feel the urge to defend against, even attack others, or at times harbor long term resentments. But if instead all of our feelings were framed as guides and reflections, useful in some way for life's journey, it would be easier to see that we are all here to learn lessons for the soul, from one another. Master life lessons are rooted in the interpersonal soul.

February 24

Each human soul is unique. There does appear to be a commonality among souls, in that this journey of lessons involves encountering painful darkness as well as loving light. As we move through life, learning each aspect of our own life's lessons helps us to move onwards towards the emotional light. By embracing and examining the dark corners of soul, the processes of life continue to move us forward.

February 25

The overall frame for this and any other kind of learning is love. This framework frees up the need to control one another so that we can better serve the higher needs of interpersonal wellness, beauty and potential that lie within interpersonal relationships. If this is not done, then we run the risk of building up clutter, leading eventually to a psychological rigidity of the spirit.

Emotional clutter breeds resentment, hatred, and prejudice. As one blames others for life's ills, there is a risk to the development of the joys of positive growth in relation to others. Over time, this kind of built up often leads us to intercultural, even heated religious or ideological warfare between inhabitants of the world.

February 26

By the honest passage through one's own pain, a fuller appreciation of what it means to learn from suffering occurs. Without this anguish, we humans would not have the knowledge and wisdom of our life's lessons. We would never know the beauty of light, joy or happiness. There is, within each of us, a defect of character or personal weakness, and a darker side. Praying and meditating to the higher loving forces of the universe, to the energy of affection that is all around us helps eliminate the worries that further drain our spirit. Instead of judging or blaming others, view them as teachers in this life. Every person we encounter (for brief or longer amounts of time) is indeed some kind of teacher for us. In some way they help us to grow and to achieve more of life's potential.

February 27

Acceptance of one's self is inextricably connected to the acceptance of others. Acceptance is a difficult process however and deeper acceptance takes work and unending attention. Spiritual acceptance connects with one's attitude toward the world, and often reflects it.

By deeply listening to others' pain and feelings, one sees that insecurity and lack of self-acceptance is indeed shared by all of us. It is in a sense a classic part of the human condition.

February 28

A more loving perspective through mindful living and acceptance of ideas with respect to others will allow love to move more freely within and between us.

A garden grows because of the condition of its soil. The human soul is a space for healthy, loving relationships to grow. The space between physical plants in a garden is just as important as the space between intimate or close relationships, and for that matter, all relationships. Relational energy between human beings is a potentially healing and sacred entity.

February 29

Love and acceptance can be nourished and nurtured through enhanced links with others. Learning from our interpersonal experiences helps us to create and appreciate, and then consider the proper conditions for growth and development.

Negativity, both within ourselves, and in relation to others, does not so much come from data or information or facts from a situation, as much as from how such facts are processed or interpreted. This is a part of our uniqueness-how we each perceive the information given to us about the world. Most of our processing styles are developed and learned through the many interactions with other people throughout our lives.

March 1

There are dramatic changes that occur once facts and information given to us are placed within a more loving context. A loving focus in our relationships opens up more positive feelings toward oneself and others. Every human being possesses an infinite amount of divine, loving energy that has the potential to transform. One has to find one's own way(s) of healing and discovering this positive life force. Focusing on past hurts or dysfunctional patterns of one's family need not keep one stuck for life or separated from positive and loving energy. Any criticism toward others, or toward oneself, runs the risk of keeping this positive energy blocked.

March 2

In this life, there is much pain and ambiguity. But there is also infinite beauty, love and the desire to change things for the better. By accepting the love of human uniqueness a pivotal process is set into motion. There are justices and injustices in life, and in our relationships with others. Positive changes occur in due time. More often than not, relationships give back what we put into them. It is difficult to stay authentic and accepting. Pain is a teacher. Ultimately we realize that in order to more deeply and meaningfully communicate with the higher forces of life we must move through the pain and learn from it. Pain deepens authenticity and humanity. It causes the intensity of our lives to develop.

March 3

There is never a full sense of peace as we move through daily forces and life's unknown lessons present themselves. Lessons are taught not by pain alone. Pain, or any other difficult process of life, is only a part of our struggle. The bigger issue is what do we do with the learning? How is it used? How does the task of experiencing pain or loss, help the soul in its spiritual journey? One can never know these deeper mysteries of life to their fullest extent, but strong clues can be obtained by going deeper and feeling the connection of the space in between our relationships with others.

March 4

In thinking of one or two of the most painful events of your life, what lessons were your teachers? What occurred? How did these lessons help you learn? How did love guide or surround you in that process, even in the distressing part of your journey? Who were the important others present with you through your pain?

March 5

There is a distinction between the stages of human development and spiritual stages of growth. Each of these types of growth, human development and spiritual progress, reflect emotional growth of a certain type. Spiritual wisdom, for example, is not the same as social development, psychomotor development, chronological age or intellectual maturity. Spiritual wisdom is something that even a very young person can have. Spiritual insights do not depend on physical ability, as another example.

Suffering, pain and hurt, especially in relation to others helps us in see how spiritual development depends upon paying close attention to interactions with, and our reactions towards, others. Socially, in everyday, normal, conscious life, it is not easy to consistently be aware of.

March 6

When someone is crying or sharing their pain on this level or some other kind of emotional vulnerability, that individual may be viewed as weak. On the other hand, someone capable of hiding or stuffing their feelings may be viewed as strong or even as handling something very well.

Notions and stereotypes that we each have about what constitutes emotional health often run counter to what emotional development requires. What does it really mean to be weak or strong? What spiritual qualities are most important? How should we express these qualities to others? How does the flow of loving energy, to and from others, work best for you?

March 7

Emotional forces, some negative in nature, if stayed in touch with for too long, can cloud the purity of an inherently divine human state. Examples of this are destructive anger, aggression, frustration or prolonged stress. Aggression did serve a purpose for us when we had to react to primitive forms of danger in our evolutionary process to survive. Aggression is an overt behavioral response that can result, if misused, in some act of destructiveness, physical or emotional.

We now however need to learn to maximize our more loving energies or our earthly resources will be wasted or used up quickly in an uncooperative or competitive fashion.

March 8

Frustration is the result of repressing or thwarting our emotional needs or interpersonal desires. Frustration is a precursor to a more damaging state of expressive anger. In and of itself, frustration does not lead to constructive resolution of conflicted or angry feelings. Stress from repeated frustrations can result in a set of complex feelings, forming over time with a pattern of reactions such as anxieties, tensions, or physical ailments. Built up, useless stress presents itself in the body and may be experienced or expressed as unhealthy anger, even physical disease. Such patterns are hardly ever constructive or have a healthy resolution, positive relief or result in getting closer to others in any kind of meaningful way.

March 9

The first step in dealing with anger is to utilize it for more healing and healthy purposes, to go back to its most pure state of feeling. For example, this means to recognize it, identify it, and then experience it fully (inwardly). In other words, in order to find the deeper levels of feeling, prepare to do a lot of emotional work. Deeper feelings have something to do with our deeper experiences, and often involve some previous hurt or loss. They may represent a deeper desire for love or happiness. Spending some quiet time to get to those deeper feelings means integrating this practice into your routine activities of the day. This whole process (through practice) can assist you in feeling more love toward others. It is well worth the time and energy that you spend doing it.

March 10

Anger is an emotional state. It is often felt in response to feeling hurt or threatened, in a physical or emotional predicament or both. If the anger is situational, that is, if it is not old anger, it may have physical manifestations such as behavioral or bodily expressions. For each individual, this behavioral pattern differs. A clenching of the teeth, pounding on something, a tightening of one's muscles, difficulty breathing, or some other combination of patterns is often present. If the anger is old as in intergenerational, inter-ethnic warfare, then it runs the risk of ingraining itself into the psyche, forming a stronghold, or fortress, thus preventing the emotional self from developing into its naturally healing state. When left alone or not worked on, this old anger tends to penetrate into the deeper layers of the psyche, leaking passive aggression, indirect hostility, profanity, hostile expressions or body postures or even more direct physical or hostile attacks. Even war.

March 11

Negative energy toward others often brings more damage and pain. This pattern may become ingrained and cyclical. The challenge is how to get rid of this kind of energy and heal the inner spirit without additional unnecessary anguish. This level of healing would bring the soul into its more normal state without harming others. Some ways of working through anger in a healthy way are to write about feelings, bring them out artistically (with clay, collages, painting or sculpture), exercising (such as with running or walking), or talking them through in a trusted atmosphere of mutuality such as with a counselor or a good friend. Any one of these methods is helpful and powerful. Other easily accessible, daily ways are mediation or prayer, or some other way of focusing, acknowledging, or thanking a higher energy force. By focusing on this higher energy source, the force of love, gentle acceptance, and forgiveness of the universe begins to wash away excess pain and allows our more loving relationships to form more thoroughly.

March 12

An appreciation of the deeper roots of our spiritual feelings, and an understanding of working with them carefully, compassionately, constructively, and lovingly, are two of the most difficult tasks of our personal and spiritual growth presented to us during this life.

Asking one's self about honest feelings and obtaining a more peaceful and more relaxed demeanor assists with this process. As one begins to let go, more healing energies form within the psyche. As one makes room and practices this kind of cleansing, there is an expanding amount of loving energy that allows for deeper feelings within the soul. Emotional energy exists in abundance in these places as well as in the spaces between one's self and others.

Pursuing the art of relating to or trusting others, as well as oneself, along with a sense of appreciation about life's lessons, are essential activities.

March 13

Guilt is another example of a shadowy feeling area. Guilt often masks anger or unresolved resentment. Such useless, overtired guilty thought patterns are difficult to break. As with any other feeling state, guilt expresses itself differently within each of us, in spite of the fact that it is a normal part of our common language of feelings. Guilt can hide low self-esteem, grief, sadness, or even itself be a byproduct of some unreasonable expectations.

Guilt serves mostly to drain the psyche and typically it does not serve any purpose in healing. It might be helpful to look at our emotional stress in order to determine if guilt is connected to any other parts of life. It takes a lot less energy for the self to ultimately let go, a key factor of interpersonal, mindful, change.

March 14

Recollect one or two painful events of life. This reflection can be a helpful method in tracing a process. Examining the memories of such an event, or events, may assist in learning to become more authentic and genuine. The light, the love that guided or surrounded this part of our journey is evident.

Emotions such as guilt are not as pure as are our other feelings. Guilt, resentment, and anger, without the work of letting go, often serve to create more negative feelings. Such dynamics feed like parasites on the spirit. In the worst case scenario, this energy turns itself inward, gets absorbed by the body, thus contributing to stress, physical pain, and disease. Instead of storing and hoarding feelings, we need to work on allowing the range of feelings to perform their healthy functioning, and then move on. There is a joy and ecstasy to the human feeling state, while stepping toward the truer self. Recognizing the delusion that misery of what is familiar can seem to feel better than the joys of newer feelings can be freeing! Exercising and experiencing more joy and love in life thus becomes a conscious choice with less effort, as the authentic self is released.

March 15

It is important to remember that if our defenses were not necessary on some level, they would not exist. Everyone exhibits defensive thoughts and behavioral patterns now and then. Sometimes they are needed, sometimes not. They may be the result of old habits and patterns and become excessively habit-forming, overly familiar. At other times, our defenses are coping mechanisms from our youth. Defenses may have been inadvertently trained to be placed into overdrive. When defense systems are in such a state of overdrive, they rob our sense of self-respect and prevent our getting adequate love from others.

Defenses may serve as emotionally deadly fortresses that take away the energy vitally needed in order to maintain health for other aspects of the self. Defenses can grow in an out of control fashion, like weeds in a garden. They may deprive you by preventing the interpersonal light and relational nutrients from reaching places where they are badly needed. Recognizing these kinds of defenses and using them to defend the self as they are needed, not to take over one's essence, is a central step toward interpersonal wellness.

March 16

What are your defense patterns? Are they useful? Are they remnants from the past, some long gone painful event of your memory? What does your defense "mosaic" look like? Listing defenses on a sheet of paper, such as anger, repression, depression, denial, guilt, intellectualization, fear, control, manipulation, judgment, daydreaming, or projecting (along with the various combined forms of these) is one way of examining your defense mosaic, or pattern. You might try drawing this in symbolic form. How and why you have used defense mechanisms in life is an important aspect of your story. Do your defenses help you get any closer to others? Do they, in any way, help your spirit to grow?

March 17

At times, it might feel awkward to go deeper within the self. But you are never alone. Human beings are born with similar psychic anatomy. We have very basic, very solid, loving and compassionate sides, with shades of individual differences. Love and a deep sense of spirituality are what draw us as members of humanity all together as a species. As we get closer to this sense of spiritual awareness and interpersonal health, we will discover a more loving, enjoyable process of life. You will feel this as well -a loving connection with others.

March 18

A state of interpersonal wellness results in the increased understanding that such a process is motivated by the deeper self. You cannot count on others to make this happen. The strongest motivation must come from one's own self. Three major points are important to remember as cognitive guides while working on interpersonal wellness:

1. Deep change takes time.
2. Realizing that as a deep psychological clearing goes on, the psyche works unconsciously as well as consciously.
3. As one comprehends newer and previously hidden feelings, some will feel uncomfortable; particularly those feelings related to sadness, anger or fear.

This is all a part of the process; it will all lead to more healing in the end.

March 19

Trying to heal on a feeling level, in relation to others, is very difficult work. While it is important to be self-aware, remember that an over-emphasis on "I-ness" can also be self-serving, self-centered, and may draw more negative energy toward the spirit. Negative energy feeds on dynamics as power, ego, gaining strength at the expense of others, feelings of being superior, getting one's individual needs selfishly met, all done at the cost of others. This narcissistic "I-ness" has no relevance to the improvement of relating to others, or in maintaining healthy, loving relationships essential for wellness. Narcissism confuses love with domination and control.

I-ness is in direct contrast to the love-focused behaviors of interpersonal wellness. Interpersonal mindfulness is focused on appreciating, and being grateful for the sanctity of our connection with others. All kinds of relationships, not only marriage, even simple daily interactions of life, are important, all sacred. Life itself is a holy process because all of the relationships here, both of a nourishing and painful nature, are teachers. All relationships are spiritually inspired. Interactions between us need to be balanced, not domineered. Forgiveness, acceptance, and the sacred flow of interaction between people should receive the highest priority of our attention. Each and every human being possesses loving and irreplaceable qualities, innately, at different moments, in various developmental stages, at distinct levels of expression throughout life.

March 20

At times, we lose contact with our mystical, loving essence, particularly if we are under some kind of unusual stress. These are the difficult moments of life for staying with any program of wellness. It is important during these times to ask for help from God, or a higher force of your understanding, to go deep within the soul to seek out, and get back on to a path of interpersonal holiness. A spiritual vessel is a wonderful thing, but, unless felt with and toward others, empty. Whatever people believe God or some higher guiding force to be, they will generally agree that this universe (as well as its lessons), often works mysteriously. It also works effectively, usually through other people encountered throughout life.

March 21

Seeking out, and finding love and balance is possible, each and every day. Encountering our fellow traveling spirits is a major part of this whole web of interpersonal energy that we all share. It surrounds our planet and connects us all in this exciting adventure. Seeking out and connecting with this loving energy source is essential. It should not to be fought off or resisted. This work goes deeper than simply a fascination with loving energy or an awareness of deeper feelings. It involves a process of closely paying attention, almost living in a meditation, with an awareness of the I-thou energy that is present in our everyday lives. As modern science discovers new physics models, the world in general seems to be noting that, in paying attention to certain phenomena, they change. These wonderful new discoveries have not been given the amount of attention they deserve in order to be maximized, spiritually or emotionally. Interpersonal healing intimately connected to the conscious and unconscious expressions of love in our daily lives. Attention impacts reality.

March 22

Attention toward going deeper and focusing more on loving energy provides an inner level of safety. This is spiritual safety. It impacts upon the psyche and gets communicated in a variety of ways, both within the self and in connection with others. Thousands of feeling states and nuances are felt during any given day. There is often no need to consistently focus on fear or anxiety. Love needs to be the consistent focus for our ultimate survival.

March 23

The mysteries of life are not a part of some paranormal spectrum. Interpersonal mysteries exist right here, right now, between and within each of us, every day. Just by looking, you can easily witness them. Whoever or whatever it is that guides us, is guiding not only humanity, but plants, birds, planes, cloud movements, intuitions, and earthly patterns of love. There is a forceful guiding impetus, there is no question.

Sometimes there is the temptation to list and label all of these mysteries as nature. But what is nature? Does nature just happen without any direction? In viewing the deeper mysteries of daily life, the normal goings on, we can observe many mysteries and miracles, in relation to others, through our instincts or intuitions, as there are many gifts surrounding us, each and every day.

March 24

Feelings can nurture our more loving side. There are numerous, latent interpersonal forms of love present in our interactions of life. To really let go is to let our deeper loving feelings surface. Tapping into this hidden, loving strength helps the inner aspect of the self. Connecting with this side means to continually cultivate it. This is well worth the time and effort. By looking more deeply, and watching carefully, nurture the uniqueness and joy of time with others. The I-thou connection is an intensely holy place. It is the pivotal resource for growing and mobilizing loving energy in your life.

March 25

By looking more mindfully, loving more deeply, you remove destruction and despair. In the zones of the purest feelings, there is no superficiality, stress or dishonesty, just a steady progression of increased energy and power of love. Healthier feelings may emerge into one's space, without obsession or control. By staying with this process, and opening up healing pathways, a lucid and more productive approach is created for spiritual wisdom and interpersonal freedom.

March 26

Allowing one's mind to grow helps the heart. Temporary stress may be a by-product of growth. But as one works, worry, guilt, prejudice and other energies may surface, and ultimately push through. They metaphorically "rinse off" from the psyche, and the psyche becomes more cleared for its real mission, which is to allow a stronger sense of centered and loving feelings to be put to use in relationships.

This occurs once the way is cleared. The quality of relationships markedly changes. Allow this love to flow freely between you and other people and remove the negative patterns.

March 27

Breathe in the loving wisdom from the universe. Discover the flow of energy that is already here. It has been here for a long time. Energy is released. It becomes apparent once blocks are removed. The rich relaxation of the soul is released, along with a knowledge that no one person is in charge of this world. The universe runs on loving energy rhythms with something far greater than anything any one of us can consciously fathom or provide. The key to interpersonal wellness is to recognize, and tap into this love, and allow its energy to flourish.

March 28

Focus on interpersonal wellness and use some of the facts of modern physics. Focusing on positive principles allows for the appreciation of the paradigms of new science and puts them into immediate use in your life.

For example, many people have learned to live in a world where logical principles apply. To learn things linearly, involving cause and effect, input and output and so on has been our standard. This kind of thinking is predominant, often mistakenly, in significant relationships, in work-related relationships, especially when dealing with feelings. Statements such as, "She makes me so sad," or "My father made me into an angry person," and "I've got to get her to stop drinking," are representative statements of such common misconceptions about the linearity of feelings with incorrect frameworks of reasoning. Feelings exist in a different universe, a relational one.

March 29

Life, particularly in this sense, is often nonlinear, or what Carl Jung called acausal. Much of what occurs and much of what is chosen in life is only a small part of an overall complex pattern, or complicated system, consisting of a mosaic of many different related and unrelated dynamics. All individuals are very complicated. Significant relationships with others are complex as well and occur on many different levels. This is true for all factors of life. In order to understand nature, or any part of it, even a tree, requires seeing that the tree as an essential and whole dynamic, an ever evolving pattern of beauty. It is not just a leaf connected to another, and then connected to a branch, or with one branch connected to another, in turn connected to its trunk. While these connections make sense, they are overly simplistic and miss an authentic and much bigger picture, the gestalt or whole, of the "tree."

March 30

Interpersonal communication occurs on a dynamic and complicated level. This is one of the many reasons why, as human beings communicate, one person may hear or see one part of the communication, and someone else, another. Each person needs to help the other understand more of the whole dynamic. By focusing on love or positive energy, a crucial step in this process is created. It sets the stage for a kind of expansion, a more holistic way of viewing of any situation. A focus on interpersonal wellness through interpersonal mindfulness facilitates deeper learning and greater mutual understanding.

March 31

Hearing a person out fully helps us to see the world in the manner that they do. By tuning in to the rhythms of that person, much positive energy is released. This involves not seeing what they are doing or what they are saying as cause and effect, or agreeing or disagreeing, but rather, hearing their words as a precious part of the overall pattern of that person's vision of this world. This kind of experience can cleanse and heal communication and the space between.

April 1

Beginning the focus of interpersonal wellness means letting go of a certain type of control. It is important to be prepared for most things in life, but having emotional expectations of others is not reasonable. We cannot take responsibility for things not within our control such as the future, problems that have not happened, other people's concerns or past situations. These dynamics can drain one's loving energy and contribute to additional mental and physical stress and fatigue. One must try to love more authentically, devotedly and meaningfully in the present with no strings or control attached to other people.

April 2

If experiencing something difficult or stressful has happened, it is essential to not pretend that it isn't happening, or to repress feelings. Be easy and gentle with yourself, and ask for loving support from others. Feeling love allows for positive potential to develop. God (or whatever you believe the guiding energy force of this universe to be) has created people in many emotional forms. In private moments or in moments of silence or reflection try and focus on this and appreciate the wealth of God's love. Put energy into loving back as well.

For whoever or whatever God may be, it is helpful to have the flow of love in both directions in order to add to the level of harmony to our universe. Mutual loving activates potentiality. More energy opens up. By tuning in more to the force of love, one automatically has more to give to others.

April 3

Impossibly high expectations are not helpful.

All human gifts are special because we are all part of a special journey through this life. The ability to fully be one's self is unique. The authentic deep potential within allows reaching down deep, and getting closer to a more loving state of being. Unique human nature is resilient, flexible and worthy of love and respect. It is sacred in its connection to the all that is. By making love happen, our higher human spirit can respond.

April 4

Positive energy and the intensity of love are around us all the time. The journey of the inner spirit lives within the emotional life. This is what gentle, emotional healing is all about. One cannot stay connected to the energy of blaming. One must stay connected to the energy of a vision, to actively and proactively seek out a more meaningful and spiritual journey. Harnessing the most inner loving spirit automatically creates a better life. In general, such harnessing allows for the clearing of a greater potential. It is a beginning on this healing road to wholeness and wellness, the listening of one's deeper loving feelings.

In those silent moments where some inner calm can be achieved, listen deeply to your spirit. Opportunities present themselves for major emotional steps toward healing.

April 5

Living life through routinely doing, or acting, results in nothing. Probing and gently poking at the psyche gives rise to one of the greatest miracles of life: emerging consciousness. Outside of us, external things draw us in, attract us, focus our attention or consciousness, and distract from this birthing process. Each of us thrives for more meaning throughout our daily life.

When we are in touch with the greater meaning of things, something greater than the normal routine of what is, a peak experience emerges leading us toward a connection toward the center of being. These moments of being fully alive through emotional birthing experiences, come with mediation, prayer, reflection, creativity, intellectual insight, or genuine I-thou encounters.

Progress, especially of an emotional and spiritual nature, is what matters. And in our universe, even the smallest act of progress has significant ramifications.

April 6

When it comes to loving energy, there is a cosmic clock at work. Our loving energy exists within infinite time. There are many types of love. How a person chooses to feel and express love in each moment of each day is a pattern that is totally unique to that person.

Love is the only reason for the spirit to be and the main reason for the spiritual life. It is the focal reason for being alive. Love, in its many forms, is a manifested energy-powered force. It is stronger than any other force. Spiritually, love matters more than anything. A deeper recognition of this fact will help to energize us. Different cultures and societies could benefit from this expanded form of love-related consciousness in relation to each other. In our social and worldly matters, if this power is ignored, then progressively deeper trouble is possible. Evolution of our species is in serious jeopardy. Love, as a powerful force, fuels not only our interpersonal relationships, but intrapersonal (within a person) energy as well as the energies of families, groups, churches, organizations, institutions, and whole cultures of our world.

April 7

When a greater focus is placed on love, its energy manifestation and inherent power increases. The level of love increases as its energy is exchanged between people. This is especially true when there are no expectations or no one wants anything in return. In other words, love increases simply by thinking about it, by feeling it in relation.

Love's momentum gathers with each act of loving behavior. Many of us have witnessed this with friends and family gatherings, meetings or groups. This is the essence of interpersonal wellness.

If you are in a group, (and it happens to be a positively energized gathering), notice how the group's involvement is far greater than any two people, or "sum" of its parts. Notice how you can feel the loving energy as it does its healing work. Each day, this focus on the positive, loving energy grows. This is the case when the focus is on the higher spirit of consciousness (the God of your understanding). This kind of positive activity and energy knows no bounds. Positive thoughts, feelings, and meditations serve to enhance this sense of well-being and contribute to an overall sense of well-being in the world.

April 8

Our loving emotions are precious processes and different for each person. In our outcome and information-driven age, our psyche is often treated as a commodity. It is no wonder that quick-fix solutions and simple answers are expected. Quick results are not possible with our human spirit. It runs on its own time and sacred guidelines. It is beyond time. Not able to compartmentalized or dichotomized, it is free, creative and God-connected.

By gently concentrating on our genuine feelings, we learn peacefully. We can inwardly examine what our feelings mean. Learning to honor them and realize that they are guides for the enhanced states of our being. Feelings help in the process of becoming more fully human and loving.

April 9

There are subtle differences between our thoughts and feelings. Our chosen or controlled states of relaxation often relate to both our thoughts and feelings. Loving thoughts integrated with our feelings can often ease our fears and tensions. Our psyche is able to experience joy, fear, sadness and anger, as guideposts, all gifts. Our spiritual lessons utilize feelings as landmarks for growth and change. And with continued daily practice, the groundwork is laid for a more abundant life filled with interpersonal wellness.

April 10

Interpersonal wellness and relational health are based on the concepts of loving detachment, non-possessive warmth, caring without control, and genuine loving.

There is no magical external force in the world that can "fix" our relational problems, our work environment or family life. Personal responsibility accounts for the changes that affect our lives. One cannot change by simply giving something or someone another name.

A label cannot possibly define all that one is, nor should it control all that one is. Labels are helpful in some ways but may also serve as blocks to having a richer knowledge of one another.

April 11

Dichotomous thinking potentially robs us of some of our individuality and may inadvertently promote prejudicial thinking. It is important to keep a balance going in life, and in relationships, not based on labels or simple explanations. Are you defined by what you do for work? Do you define yourself according to your race, sex, IQ? These factors about one's self are each a part of overall identity, but the total self is much more than any part. Any one person is more than the sum of his or her labeled aspects, more than any one classification.

April 12

Authentically connecting with others is very rewarding. Relational bonds are a centerpiece of spirituality. Connecting goes beyond being simply associated through physical intimacy or a powerful physical attraction. Genuine intimacy goes beyond words: It is more transcendental than tribal. Intimacy is a spiritual adventure that speaks not in a language but in the language of the soul. It is not exactly neither sexual nor physical yet it may include aspects of each. It is the I-thou adventure, the recognition that there is indeed a spirit in connection, the recognition that spirit is always hard at work in life, each time one meets and relates to another person.

April 13

Meeting another person, another soul, or spirit, and discovering what is shared in this exchange is far greater than the simple immediate contact of the moment, or the defined context of the situation. Giving way to one another's loving soul is the essence of what is captured in a here and now encounter, who and what you are in relation. The loving energies of the spirit emerge.

The recognition of this allows us to see that a higher intelligence exists. This recognition of love, beauty, and intuitive connection, helps to build interpersonal patience, acceptance, positive energy, and synergistic feelings in living each day more fully. In short, this facilitates more healthy and healing bridges of energy between one another. This, in turn, helps us to achieve the dream of becoming and being more transcendental and peaceful and less tribal or war-like people.

April 14

In this world, each person is a unique individual and each of us in one-to-one or group settings creates relational bonds that are distinctive each day. This exceptional spiritual bond exists as it does only in a given moment. Even when such a bond may feel unhealthy or fraught with conflict, there is often a spirit driven purpose or lesson of the heart present. Such a relationship is a teacher of spiritual energy, with some kind of an interpersonal message involved. There are millions of these types of bonds present at any given time in our universe of relational being. There is a preponderance of relational energy in our world, an unbelievable amount of interactive energy. In relation to love, all that is around us has not been fully tapped into.

April 15

Life is made up of numerous interactions, whole networks of people helping to define who we are and who we become as we live. Each of us has access to the human network of warmth, compassion, and interpersonal respect. The work of each of us matters in this world. One's own identity and being grows through paying of attention to relational health. Our work heals those places where not enough intimacy exists, or has not had an opportunity to adequately develop.

April 16

Intimacy may not lead to an actualized physical or sexual action. Intimacy can lead to a creative, sensitive or powerful sensation of being in the world. Examine this kind of force in your life with such questions as: What are those qualities, those experiences, those memories, activities, that I consider "intimate?" Or, with who does this kind of love focused intimacy happen in my daily life? Even for brief moments, seconds, in an immediate encounter, where are the strong feelings? It is easy at times to lose one's sense of excitement about life, be it about one's self, other people, or one's situation. It is easy to lose this in the haste of a daily schedule of activities. Yet intimacy is the power source of interpersonal wellness.

April 17

It is easy to get caught up in the need to do something in this externally driven and oriented world. Unconsciously there is an obvious and greater mystery of meaning in our source of humanness. This is the case, especially, emotionally and spiritually.

An inner desire for connecting with others often motivates our behaviors. When this inner desire is negatively affected or minimized by external forces, or the perceived importance of the opinions of others (or other false distractions of the external material world), there is the risk of alienation, addiction and emotional despondency, among other things.

April 18

The authentically human, innate, inner excitement of life is sustained by the recognition of awareness. Daily expectations of the interpersonal spirit come from whatever is creatively desired form the unique emotionality of spirit, alone, or in connection with others. Awareness of awareness builds depth in connection with others. Addressing it openly with another builds it even more.

April 19

The words, or the phrase, "being in recovery" may ring a familiar tone for some. In a sense, each of us needs to recover one's own self, one's authentic nature, in this life. This is true whether or not there is any specific identification of an addiction, or problem. The challenge of life involves finding and nurturing the authentic and healing spirit within one's self and in relation to others.

April 20

In a sense, each spirit is living as a distinct interactive soul in our culture. There is a risk of an emotional and spiritual state of unawareness of one's fullest capabilities, if unaware of interpersonal mindfulness. At times this involves a choice to put painful feelings on hold, say, from a difficult past or childhood. One can recover from a painful past. One can recover a sense of fulfillment, wonder, actualization and appreciation of life. The notion of recovery awaits each of us in this sense. How can an inner, creative, individual "spark" be more fully developed in your life? How can you learn to visualize a more complete, loving, cherished and authentic life?

April 21

In today's society, overwork, stress, and over-achievement are common themes. They are highly valued by certain segments of our society. This kind of "busy-ness" unfortunately interferes with our authentic living. Feeling overwhelmed is a great impediment to personal growth and development. The best way to deal with any of these counterproductive forces is through prevention. A prevention program would nurture the spirit adequately in a context of interpersonal mindfulness.

There are many tools available to develop a prevention program, such as self-help programs, counseling, positive relationships, spiritual practices, and meditation. They can be used as long as one keeps in mind the balanced perspective of achieving harmony in one's daily relationships is the major, guiding principle of life.

April 22

By focusing and putting more energy into this guiding principle, one can prevent the kinds of stressors that lead to an obstructed level of progress and development. Another way to prevent painfully stressful situations is by making it a priority to share energies with others in a more loving, give-and-take fashion. If one plans this attentively, then a more self-caring and balanced life develops.

A prevention program would help, for example when there is an unusual amount of stress, or major life changes going on. One cannot expect everything to go right in abnormal circumstances such as these. These are the types of situations that call for learning and applying a new set of self-caring skills.

April 23

In determining preventive behaviors to deal with stress, time is necessary in order to fully absorb what one needs. Allow special time and some meaningful moments of reflection for yourself. Take a relaxing bath or listen to some healing music. Learn to let go and detach from things from which you have no control or little influence. These can build up on any given day. The situation in our world politically, aspects of someone else's personality; someone else's family situation; are all examples of things over which we have little or no control.

Fretting over such matters needlessly causes stress, inner irritation, leaving us vulnerable to substance and relational addictions. Letting go, while it requires intensive work, wastes not nearly the same amount of energy as hanging on. The more energy one has to give to others; more quality time emerges for energizing activities, creativity, positive interactions, working, and quality loving.

April 24

What does "enabling" really mean? It is an interesting exercise to note the different levels of energy when you are enabling as opposed to lovingly detaching. Notice how it feels when you are emotionally drained. Notice what is going on outside of you and within you. Emotional drainage is a sure sign of control or enabling. Having more available energy is a sign that you are learning to let go of enabling and appropriately and lovingly detach. Detachment and an appreciation for the moment, of what is, are simple yet difficult to work on. It involves being your true or authentic self, bringing a sense of working spirituality into your life. Choices and relationships need to be adjusted to the ways of loving detachment, but eventually these areas of life adjust to this new way of being.

April 25

Closeness with others in life is desired by most of us. The skills for obtaining a better quality of closeness are largely untapped and underdeveloped. How we can be so technologically advanced yet at the same time able to destroy one another's' communities, societies and ways of life in the flash of an instant? It is time to encourage heightened objectives of positive health to achieve our sense of emotional development. It is an ambitious goal to pursue, individually and collectively. There are skills that can be taught and learned related to these aims. It is possible that we can learn interpersonal proficiencies more extensively in our schools, churches and communities. There can hardly be a more urgent agenda for the world.

April 26

Closeness, love, and trust have different meanings for each of us. Imagine how our world would change if such interpersonal concepts were more defined, expressed and actualized. Even simple visualizations, on a step by step, individual level, create positive changes for the larger world. Practicing visualization skills is one example of how energy is power and energy is matter. The power for change is an inherent ability that has been given to each and every one of us. We can, through practice, have consistent and cumulative, positive effects upon one another.

April 27

In establishing the process of visualization, any achievement is possible. This involves taking risks. It may mean a temporary feeling of loss. It means reaching out to others, with all of your weaknesses and strengths. With an emphasis on this kind of effort, building effective, foundational functionality receives more attention in our lives.

April 28

There is a lot about us, individually, and in groups, that is functional and effective. There is a lot to be said for what is done right each day! There is a need to build on what constitutes a more functional and healthy emotional self. To build this means taking chances in the direction of becoming closer to others, in a more genuine way, especially to people whom you love and care about the most.

April 29

If you were to select three people that mean the most to you in life, do you think that these people would be aware that you selected them? Would there be some way in which you can let any, or all, of them know how you feel about them? Our lives are so fragile and dear. It's important in the here and now, to acknowledge this, not after our loved ones have passed on.

Many people carry around heavy emotional expectations. There are events we expect to happen, or that we think "should" happen, or, if something is done, then there will be, or should be an automatic reaction to it. For example, in doing something nice for someone (such as a neighbor or friend) there may be an anticipation that someday it will be reciprocated or something similar will be done for you. True caring, however, that which is unconditional in nature, carries with it no such expectations.

April 30

Assumptions are dangerous, unless they have been openly talked about, agreed upon, and work in a healthy way for everyone involved. Paying someone a compliment, or favor, unexpectedly, and preferably, anonymously, results in a tremendous feeling. To expect nothing in return is one of life's greatest gifts. Actions such as this may become a more established way, life without any attached strings or expectations of others to meet our needs.

May 1

Thoughts are as important as feelings and behaviors. They all work together in different combinations. Behaviors are the outward evidence for areas that matter most to us. By observing all three, thoughts, feelings and behaviors, we can learn a great deal. Observation skills are an important part of our daily life. Understanding our behaviors is also essential in order to grow individually and together.

May 2

Observing one's way of being in the world is a constructive way to set in motion improving our behavioral styles. What are your "typical behaviors" on a given day? Which of your behaviors have been positive? Which have been unhelpful? Which of your behaviors seem to cause stress? What are some behavioral plans for improvement that could be undertaken?

May 3

It is easy to be perplexed by differing viewpoints presented to us about religion, money, or relationships. One simple example dealing with the expression of feelings illustrates this. There are many possible opinions about feelings, yet, all feelings, or any one feeling, could easily be selected. Consider your most basic philosophical stance about feelings. What do you believe is their purpose? Why do we have feelings? Are they necessary for the learning of spiritual lessons? Are they developmental or holistic viewpoints across the life span, indicative of the stages of our human development? Could it be any one of these purposes, or some combination of all of them? No wonder it is easy to become so confused as to the nature and meaning of feelings! Each of these viewpoints is useful, but one must discover the importance of finding one's own inner values about feelings, and what these ideals mean in this life, especially in relation to your own spiritual lessons. It is worth exploring this further. What are the happiest moments of your life and why were they happy? What was the role of your feelings in these situations? How were they used to help you?

May 4

Most of us understand the effects of narcissism, or self-centeredness and the related risks and negative implications towards others. An extreme level of self-centeredness is obviously not a good thing. It often leads to emotional damage and dysfunction-both for the narcissist and his or her various significant others. It is a condition that has emotionally toxic effects for the spirit. What is narcissism's antidote, spiritually? Learning how to improve our giving love to others, through mindfully practicing this feeling on a daily basis, whenever possible is the hopeful interpersonal antidote. Practicing the principles of interpersonally mindful living in order to develop a more positive approach and nourishing environment creates an enhanced state of being. It makes life more an enjoyable sojourn.

May 5

There are too few words in this world for love, yet there are the many kinds of adoration that we experience. The ancient Greek culture had words for instinctive love, brotherly love, friendship, passionate love and sexuality; and for the deep love of worthiness and human respect. One of the most irrational and unrealistic norms that we place upon ourselves is the sense of feeling that it is okay to not focus upon love in its varied form in our experiences in this world. This norm is learned, as we become more sophisticated or as our inner being becomes more disengaged or discouraged. This way of being may also originate from a fear of coming across too selfishly or too vulnerably. The reality is that we all can connect to love.

May 6

We need to acknowledge the many forms of love. We have more names for illnesses, pathologies, car parts and computers that we do for this powerful universal force. We need to proactively create a forum for interpersonal mindfulness. We need to challenge our social programming and established interpersonal norms or behaviors. There is a need to develop beyond this, beyond our unhealthy expectations, and tap into the potential that we each possess in order to be our highest loving selves. Loving authentically in a spiritual way transcends behavior.

May 7

As more of us practice these principles of interpersonal wellness, an energy force will take place capable of moving us forward. Old patterns would likely be broken. Prayer, meditation, conscious forgiveness, and the listening for the deeper rhythms of life and love, will serve as catalysts for the state of interpersonal wellness to grow more effectively. A good place to begin this pattern of interpersonal mindfulness in this systematic way is with one's self.

May 8

Hurt feelings, over time, transform into deep-seated resentments or even destructive anger. One must forgive one's self for this and realize that engaging in new patterns of life is possible. Shifting them can begin at any time. It is important to learn new ways of behaving, both within one's self, and in relation to others, with a gentle style.

May 9

By focusing in a conscious way, a powerful energy is released, as we have discussed. This is the essence of interpersonal wellness and interpersonal mindfulness. By focusing more consciously on this energy an improved mental state emerges, in most situations, either in relation to one's self or others. Focusing sets into motion more opportunities to create loving feelings and to observe the connections of love all around us. One's ability to be a receiver or conductor of loving feelings improves. It becomes apparent that love is an energy force, more than an emotion. It has the power to change things. It is a potent source that we minimally tap into.

May 10

The forces of love, in order to be activated in more powerful way, require our conscious help and less of our imagined fears. This must begin as soon as possible. Our peaceful and gentle inner natures are more dominant than we realize. We are ready to grow in more ways.

Achieving better communication between people is one of the biggest hurdles that face us in this process. It is one of the major issues that counselors, couple and family counselors, priests, and teachers hear about in their work-communication blocks. Improving our communication skills would no doubt help with the aforementioned issues and on a grander scale would also help us evolve into a more loving species.

May 11

When attempting to assess our overall communication problems our issues can be a bit overwhelming. It is better to break the sum total of issues down into smaller parts or behaviors, verbally and nonverbally. The nonverbal area is more difficult to work on.

Tone of voice, body posture, the ability to concentrate and look someone in the eye, to be there while communicating with them, are all extremely difficult behaviors to assess.

They are difficult to practice, but it can be done!

May 12

Social interaction is an important aspect of nonverbal communication. Our lives can easily be influenced by others. This is often influenced by backgrounds, styles, cultures, community, and personality patterns. One's hidden observer is a powerful force and can assist us in identifying and recognizing many different nonverbal patterns of communication.

It is important to make this kind of commitment to change one's self, and to genuinely value others more. Learning to be mindful, paying close attention, and lovingly focusing on our communication skills creates love, and gives it away, again and again.

May 13

With this kind of process, the daily, external world changes in that it becomes more of a mirror, reflecting the larger sense of peace growing within us. Life becomes gradually and gently, a wonderful series of opportunities to become more authentic and loving. Affection grows. It always grows with this kind of work. This is love's natural state, currently repressed. It is we who stifle it, unknowingly and unwittingly. Both verbal and nonverbal communication naturally deepens as more love is released. Relationships are enhanced and become more enjoyable.

May 14

Love is a powerful interpersonal force that integrates our physical, emotional, intellectual and spiritual states of being. Love is the cement that holds all of this together and indirectly holds all aspects of our human family together. Love is the great connector.

We live our lives with love as our guide, yet it is often difficult to utter the word. This is so even in academic and health care circles, where we have learned and verified that love is essential to health and recovery.

May 15

Another good example of loving synergy is in the use of our analytic skills. Thinking, or the natural human ability to think, is an extremely useful skill that can be utilized effectively. This ability is essential to our survival as a species. Yet we do not often associate our survival as a species with the further development of love.

May 16

Observe your inner thoughts as they work, without judging others or yourself. Simply focus on the essence of others, as well as what is.

This is an especially useful exercise to try with another person and then to spend some time talking about it.

Select ten things that you love deeply be they people, places, things, or even aspects of the inner psyche or internal life. Keep these thoughts in mind for the day as you observe around you. Focus your attention on them.

Loving forces may become quickly activated in your daily life.

May 17

Focusing on interpersonal mindfulness is essential in order to see the bigger force, the strength of love, and to activate ways of behaviorally practicing it in the best ways possible in order to encourage its growth and to elicit more energy for the world. By inwardly practicing these principles, one cannot help but to begin to see the numerous positive effects in the external world.

May 18

Our inner lives have characteristics not unlike what is created when we toss a pebble into a pond. The force of energy creates ripples, with numerous, positive, and unpredictable effects, as they surround one's life. This is evident in the world of our psyches, both in the conscious and unconscious realms. It is clear that love rules. It is scary and exciting to meaningfully recognize this growth. When we recognize that we are not in charge of everything, and we cannot elicit or control the behaviors or thoughts of others we are freed up to feel less stress.

May 19

There are three critical areas of our lives that require the development of love-focused attention:

#1: Our needs, wants and expectations from others. This area has particular relevance in the seeking and expressing of positive intimacy in our lives.
#2: Our objective observations of our relationships with others and their reactions to us.
#3: Our genuine reactions to other people in a less controlling and more loving way.

These areas deal with closeness in one form or another and with intimacy. Each one may make us more vulnerable and open to distortions and misinterpretations. Closeness seems at times to translate into approval, and this equating of the two concepts, closeness and approval, may not be helpful.

May 20

Intimacy translates into sexuality for some people. Unfortunately, this is a message that comes from the mass media, movies and novels. We need to realize that there are other forms of intimacy, especially in the spiritual sense. There needs to be more attention to detail, discussion and education around this important issue. While this area is fraught with risk, positive changes are indeed conceivable and well worth the effort.

May 21

Examine what your actual and realistic interpersonal needs potentially consist of.

Observe what actually happens daily with other persons, significant people. What is your intimate communication like? What is its character? What are its relevant patterns?

How can you change some of the ways of behaving in relation to others; particularly in the sorting out of your assumptions and intentionally, formal clear, direct, and healthier styles of communication?

May 22

With this recognition, it is important to realize that one has a right to be a unique and devoted expression of the higher spirit of your understanding, consistent with your unique personality. Your true nature need not depend upon the judgments of others. You need to be who you are and fully accept yourself and your particular pathway of interpersonal wellness. Look down within yourself. Look deeply. Every quality of spiritual goodness exists within you.

May 23

You have attributes such as forgiveness, love, loyalty, honesty, compassion, humility, kindness, patience, a tolerance toward others, and so on. There is a unique pattern and quality of these attributes that are yours and that embrace your world each time they are practiced.

It is amazing to begin to see these miracles of everyday life. In peoples' voices, animals, the patterns of the leaves, the multitude of variations in nature's designs. Seeing life's journey and cultivating compassion in everyday life is a real possibility-anywhere, anytime, every waking moment, even in the smallest ways. For even in those small ways, it is the little things, that truly connect us and that people often remember.

May 24

By engaging more fully in unplanned acts of kindness, appreciation of one's self and others deepens. Daily respect, ethical interpersonal behaviors and more focus on kindness builds up the spiritual condition of our human race. The feelings of mutuality with other souls, comes back and recycles, many times over, especially when it is not so easy to forgive and make amends and move beyond the battles run by ego and fear.

May 25

Through taking the time to notice the deeper spiritual beauties of life, interactions with others become energized. Taking note of what creates specific positive energy intensifies the emotional energy and the whole spirit. By focusing on the many wonders of life and of its creations, the heart of it all manifests more plainly.

Everyone is an active carrier of interpersonal prosperity. Even though everyone alive today very likely has experienced pain or hurt, and nearly everyone has come from a family system that has somewhat suffered, (it is obviously part of the nature of life to suffer), each of us also bears the potential for infinite love. Each person, each family system is unique. And systems, just as individuals, are creative and loving organisms capable of so much more.

May 26

Sometimes suffering occurs in life around some specific trauma. Different things constitute trauma to different people. The drama of our existence is rooted in uniquely experienced, phenomenological events. There are obvious, painful, external traumas that affect families and individuals in life and a host of subtle and tortuous internal dynamics that are at times not easily visible. There is no doubt that suffering is a teacher, a master teacher for us all.

May 27

There are many subtleties in life. Spiritual dramas need to be respected as the master teachers that they are. Verbal abuse, emotional intolerance, narcissism, undiagnosed mental illness, control dramas, neglect, oppression, prejudice—are all powerful negative energy flows that can block a realization of the positive and loving or nurturing energy that flows within a family system, or any system for that matter.

May 28

In one's own life, begin to recognize the deeper positive aspects that have emerged from traumas. What are the effects of your traumas? What can be done? How can you recognize this journey as a creative and unique one? How can you help it to be all that it is, even with all of its suffering, and, help lay the foundation for a newly healed life, based on interpersonal wellness?

May 29

An uplifting fact is the recognition that human love cannot be overpowered by anything else in the larger scheme of life. It even transcends death. Negativity, suffering, misuse of technology, hurt, intolerance, cannot, alter its power, force, or natural course. Its spiritual power cannot be measured. It is too powerful, creatively run, and interactive. Having compassion, even for oneself, and recognizing the deeper, loving, spiritual essence of relationships leads to a higher awareness and enhanced level of compassion on so many levels that fear of anticipated hurts dissolves. This leads to deeper levels of acceptance toward oneself and others. It also leads to a deeper forgiveness for life's pain, and a deeper feeling of forgiveness for the darker side of humanity.

May 30

Relationships, both painful and nurturing, are gifts. They are the connections to a more divine state. All human encounters are sacred. Each conscious thought, each meditation, each beginning of the day needs at least one moment of recognition of our many blessings. Daily times for focusing on the loving relatedness between others, can, step-by-step, build a more loving world, and it is as important, at least, as the one day we usually formally allot for a thanksgiving. Thinking more deeply of this kind of wisdom, builds love, between all neighbors, friends, strangers on the streets, between our children, the world's children, and the citizens of tomorrow. In this new millennium, interpersonal wellness is a necessary state of being. Love is the only force that can carry us on through, to a higher place of consciousness, and a higher level of evolution.

May 31

By practicing love, and consciously learning with others, we can transcend to a new place. Recognition of love, identification of its many forms, an awareness of its awareness, and its subsequent, daily expression, all are crucial steps for building interpersonal wellness, and progressively becoming a part of a concentrated state of interpersonal mindfulness.

June 1

To maintain an attitude of interpersonal wellness, think of your being in the world as a total person--physically, mentally, spiritually, and emotionally. Your being involves all of these levels. There is an immense capacity for loving and connecting with others on each and every one of these levels.

June 2

Interpersonal wellness is a holistic and contextual concept. Our landscapes as well as nature and the flow of light, have a lot to teach us about the context of emotional change. They speak to us in the language of the unconscious. In the beginning, changing one's inner emotional landscapes is a lot like doing sculpture- we chip away, stand back, observe ourselves from different levels and perspectives, let the change deepen, observe the energy with the form, watch its various levels of animation, interact with the light around it. Within every individual psychic landscape, there is a language of deeper form, of deeper communication, an unendingly, solidly placed, sacred and persisting love. This is the language of the psyche and such is the quality of the language of tuning into our higher essence and mission.

June 3

The basic nature of universal and symbolic light often has a hard time reaching us, deep within our lives and hearts. At first, this awareness of love's powerful and metaphorical light is difficult to grasp. It is in the subtle shafts of light between the darkness that help our psyche take form. What may, at first, have appeared scary or ugly, or a formless entity without potential, with the light, seems to be something entirely different with an ability to grow, with continuous and ongoing flowing potential. This is the nature of interpersonal wellness.

June 4

Try to take in fully and tune into regularly, the creativity of interpersonal wellness that already exists in your life. Observe some art work, or work of nature or decorations that you have chosen for your home, your yard, or that which exists at work or in the center of your city or town. Observe art acknowledged in your community by visiting a museum or art department at a local university, local high school or vocational school. Visit a library and observe the art history books, or art work available in other books on display there, or just go to a bookstore and browse, (or purchase) a book on art forms, sculpture or creativity. Allow the visual messages to unconsciously, calmly, in a relaxed state, be absorbed through your whole self: physically, mentally, emotionally and spiritually. The mind cannot help but to transform.

June 5

Work of our unconscious psyche, as that of the psyche of creative individuals, unearths strong common patterns and themes. One obvious theme is the authentic appreciation of the natural, loving patterns of the world. It is not difficult to capture positive feelings related to these themes. Another pattern is the deep sense of wonder concerning the obvious mystery surrounding our lives. It is difficult to not feel more reflective when noticing all of this. Another major theme concerning the creative life is that, our arrival or departure here is not as critical as the journey we live. The process is at least if not more important as the result. This factor alone should give us pause enough to slow down and consider our own, individual manner of living, yet it is very difficult especially given the number of daily goals we set ourselves up to achieve.

June 6

Moving through life as a transition is more powerful than its outcome or any one, final decision or accomplishment that we make. The how of our lives is more important than its what. At the end of life, how we treated others is more important than what we earned, in the material sense. One's process as a person is more important. Being in love with the process can carry this to a healing place of inner adventure. This higher state is transcendent and spiritual, and connects us all as human beings.

June 7

It is the love of the search, the love of the mystery that is the essence of interpersonal wellness. It means seriously take the plunge toward a more love-focused existence, to enjoy the experience, to not be afraid or it. The accompanying higher forces of the universe are always with us, especially in moving towards a direction that is consistent with its natural flow of loving energy. Being in love with the process of all that is takes us to those inner places we may have not visited since our childhood. This work leads us toward a path that is the loving power of the universe in a new way.

June 8

Another specific method would be to try to remember something in life that had a profound effect upon you in a positive way. This "something" could be a person, place or thing. Was this a loving process? If so, how? What was different from regular, everyday communication? What can be learned from this experience of how to create more healing and loving moments and experiences in your life?

June 9

Moments in life that matter most are those when people are existing in this state of interpersonal mindfulness. Those moments are dominated by feelings of love, be it for another person, idea, place or thing. By mentally listing areas where energy similar to this exists, begin a process of activating and fostering this energy. By acknowledging the memories and potentials of love, more love is unleashed; the potential for interpersonal wellness is thus endless.

In other words, miraculously, just by thinking of the positive flow, or outcomes of love, just by this simple act of focusing on it, or on those positive people or things in a more loving way, accelerates the process. The acknowledgment elicits interpersonal wellness and causes loving energy to expand. It expands from its previous state of compression, and grows in a phenomenal way. Most exciting of all is its synergistic effect upon others. The gift of interpersonal wellness is in the giving away of energy and its related synergistic effects for other people.

June 10

As strange as they may seem, time outs can be helpful for placing some of these loving thoughts and feelings into an even clearer perspective. Time-outs, or gentle and carefully planned, cleared-out, brief breaks, allow reprieve from the intensity of the day and to recharge. It allows one to breath out some of the compressed affect of the day's stress, so that there will be more room to breathe in love and create more interpersonal wellness. This processing allows for a more emotionally replenished psyche, before moving on to the next phase. The relaxing moments found in these time-outs, are different from being stuck. It is a process of gentle self-care.

June 11

An important foundation is established for the next challenge, the next tests, whatever or whenever they are presented to you, for surely they will come. They always do. No one can judge what goes on inside of you or another. No other living human being, at this point, knows more about your psyche than you. So diving boldly into your own essence and reclaiming one's self, automatically transforms this authentic nature into a more deeply loving and energized entity. Feelings serve as guides, giving us a renewed sense of self perspective and greater access to positive and loving meaning in connection with others. This capability already exists deep inside each of us, dormant, not fully nurtured.

June 12

One can feel this difference between complacency and being stuck, or this flowing, positive, love-focused feeling. What the time outs and rest periods offer is a deeper recognition of this difference. The internal differences felt in each of these states remains distinct. By listening deeply, today and every day, we can learn a great deal about these different states. And by listening to one's own feelings, our trusted, internal teachers, we can more effectively hear the loving sounds of others.

June 13

Changing our mental energy creates change. Love created from our mental energy can impact positively and transform things, simply by focusing with enhanced levels of mindfulness. This is an essential and foundational principle of interpersonal wellness and not as strange and trite an idea as it may at first seem. In fact, this seems to be a major operating principle of our universe. Attention breeds growth: This is evident even in our household plants as we focus more attention upon them; attention in and of itself often breeds improved levels of interpersonal health. This is also true with our children, family members, friends, just about anyone with whom we regularly interact.

June 14

In order to propel some our emotionally prosperous energy to any organism chosen, spend some time doing just this, with regular daily persistence. Watch the quality of progression over time. Positive energy breeds positive relationships. At times, to change, means, at first, to think differently, and to think differently reflects positive levels of feeling that in turn noticeably affect the organism in question. And, of course, usually this results in better health, all-around, for both parties involved.

June 15

To think more lovingly in one's life is like living in a state of prayer or constant meditation of the emotional realms of life. For example, in exercising the mind to positively focus on more on these areas of loving fruition, a more natural and integrated way of life yields results with family members, friends, coworkers and neighbors. By placing good, solid, mental energy outward in such a loving way, one reaps positive energy in numerous unexpected ways. At the very least, there is nothing to lose, since by focusing more on the positive energy, we create more healthful conditions for the mind.

June 16

How long has it been since you have expressed a positive attitude toward something specific in your life in a uniquely creative way? By nurturing your levels of activity creatively, a more loving element of living is cultivated. A creative outlet is also a love-focused inlet, since it appreciates one's individual and unique spirit. This means not necessarily being or feeling like a creative genius, gifted person, or artist, but simply the creative essence of one's self. This type of focusing has nothing to do with judging or assessing artistic abilities, but more with the essence of the higher self. Each and every person possesses this kind of creativity. It is a unique source that no one else can access.

June 17

We are each born with a profound creative nature within us, more so than we realize. This can be the source of our chosen form of spirituality, or, for our unique ability to transform our insights into action. It is at the heart of human spiritual change. How we connect with others, how we relate to others or to nature and the outside world, how we uniquely see things, and a whole host of other creative abilities, are all interrelated. Even something more traditionally creative like picture taking, painting, sculpture, or poetry connects to these deep areas. As long as you realize, and it bears repeating, that your goal is not to become a Van Gogh or Emily Dickinson and that the whole point is to create love, have fun, and let the full range of your creative energy flow.

June 18

There is a seed within each of us that wishes to express itself and grow creatively. If this seed is thwarted, this can cause us stress or tension, even alter our emotional health and produce repeated strain. It is important to allow time for something creative, blocking out any consideration of needing to be perfect at the creative activity. It should be something simple that helps you to feel more connection with your creative side. If it is finger painting, for, example, pay close attention to your innermost feelings at the time of engaging in this activity and attempt to be mindful and meditative about it. Get a sense of your innermost exhilaration and clear away residual stress.

June 19

Being at ease with oneself requires a deep-rooted sense of trust, especially with all that exists on this earth. This can be much more difficult than it might at first seem. There is a lot of fear associated with being more honest with being oneself, especially with others. How much is fear of how others see us? What kinds of feelings truly and genuinely generate love in your life? Is there a fear that your genuine feelings will overtake or control others? Feelings are one small part of what makes a human being whole. Feelings are our guides, and one's makeup is greater than the sum of its various parts, whatever those parts might be-feelings, thoughts, or behaviors.

June 20

It is important to ask ourselves what is the value of conditional love? Of what use is love if it is conditional? Conditional love is an oxymoron: The concept of love has little meaning if one is loved with any strings attached. Review, either by writing down, or just mentally to one's self, what specific fears are in your life, especially in relation to others.

Become more honest and gradually it becomes easier to be open. A closer more authentic bond with close friends, spouses, partners, or family members helps us to face our fears. By working them through, fears are minimized and make room for a more complete self to arise.

June 21

Mental challenge and creative growth are two areas of life that can be easily blocked. We believe that time devoted to any such endeavor as creative growth is a luxury. This cultural bias often prevents the development of further potential in this area.

There are many different types of intelligence that we each possess: academic, creative, interpersonal, physical, spiritual, and various combinations thereof. Each of us is blessed with some kind of a unique constellation, or mosaic of intelligence. It is impossible to compare, or accurately measure intelligence, between people. It is important to examine just what type of individual intelligence exists, and to then nurture it, gently, steadily, carefully. Through listening to music, or in doing crossword puzzles, math problems, praying, reading, and generalized observing, we can further nurture our unique intelligence.

June 22

Creativity, as a form of intelligence, can be nurtured by painting something- walls, finger painting, oil painting, sculpturing, clay, or even by simply walking on a beach. Sitting on a street corner or at a mall, and just watching other people is also a creative endeavor; even popping corn is creative! Nurture your mind and heart in whatever your intuitive inner places seek. This will assist you in the enrichment of your unique intelligence development. Here is a sample list of suggested activities to help with this process. Any one of these activities, mindfully done, will assist in the promotion of prosperous energy:

o Taking a class
o Having a good talk with another person, a nurturing conversation
o Intensively observing something
o Going to the movies
o Reading anything
o Learning some new information
o Shopping for a new book
o Learning a new skill
o Attending a cultural event
o Listening intently to your thoughts
o Visiting and browsing around on the campus of a local college
o Visiting a local park
o Playing a game
o Really touching something while concentrating on it
o Going for walk
o Visiting a mall
o Visiting a zoo

June 23

As a whole person who is more than the sum parts, you are connected to others by a deep love for all things and this binds together your mind, body, and spirit as a whole entity. It is likely though that some of your "parts" are overused on a daily basis, and it is also least likely that this part or any part is as powerful as your whole spirit, or human essence. If any one part, say the brain, is treated, as one's true essence, or your whole self, then the essence of the total self is thwarted and risks under development. This kind of imbalance can be caused by a whole host of situational events, such as overwork, parenting, or crisis situations. Through stopping and thinking about this, a kind of quick internal, emotional "cat scan" of your life can be a helpful activity, a housecleaning of sorts, or inventory, of your emotional and spiritual states. How much balance is there? Surprisingly, there are simple, yet effective steps to take in order to seek out more balance and equilibrium of your whole self, and to heal from, say, the areas of overwork or burnt out energy levels, or any other imbalances of overuse and abuse. Examine the following areas from a healing and spiritual perspective, as one method for this process. How much time and energy do you typically spend in each area?

o   With a hobby or interest
o   In positive relationships
o   Using your special skills
o   Social activities
o   Outdoor activities
o   Improving your health
o   Quiet time

June 24

Ponder upon a relationship with something greater than one's self. These are often minor areas that comprise some of our peak spiritual gifts in life. If nothing else, at the very least, focus for a moment on the spontaneity of your spiritual essence, and just be there. This is a way of taking a mental vacation without actually physically going anywhere. It means placing into practice the concept of loving detachment, or letting go of any external, material stress for a few precious moments. It takes some focusing but, once attained, this process will allow you the feeling of spiritual nourishment, and in many ways, a more relaxed state than an actual vacation can -certainly costing less money, taking less energy, and less actual physical preparation! An even longer kind of vacation is possible by giving oneself more nurturing sleeping experiences, healthier food, more positive people around, cleansing of physical and emotional toxins, engaging in positive activities, and working on creating positive conscious thoughts. This clearing away activity elicits more feelings of calmness and relaxation. And once again, they are powerful examples of how by just focusing on some positive mental energy in a certain direction, we can nurture other aspects of the self, quickly and synergistically. Most methods of authentic self improvement do not require a lot of money or fancy methodology. They can, and ideally should, be practiced right at home or during one's daily routine, with people whom you trust.

June 25

Self-improvement is not of any worth unless authentically integrated within your daily life. Most barriers to our plans for self-improvement are our everyday life and routines. During our conscious waking life, such barriers often create tension, and this tension can be used as a helpful barometer for you in further identifying these blocks. The barricades are not frequently anything mysterious, invisible, or unknown. Most of these barriers, at least the ones during our conscious waking hours, are specific behaviors.

June 26

As one first notices and gets prepared to remove any blocks, it is important to ask: When, or where, is the tension? How does it feel and where is felt? In the mind? A certain part of the body? In the heart? Feelings? Is it a mental, emotional, interpersonal, spiritual, or physical tension? Is it felt in the body mind, in free flowing thoughts? Is it in some combination of these areas? Try, for a moment, to think especially about which qualities others find relaxing about you. After this task is completed, think about what area you feel most strongly about. What area needs change? Where is your working energy on a given day? Are there discrepancies between what is ideally done and what is actually done? What can be done about this kind of discrepant situation? Because of our discrete uniqueness, there are no easy answers to what it would be like to become more emotionally well on any level of our being. Some of us have a powerful physical side, and with proper nurturance and additional strength, this can spill over in positive way into other areas, such as our emotional side. Health from each area can be visualized as spreading and have useful, positive influences upon other aspects of the self.

June 27

There is no doubt that one's feeling state can be nurtured by physical activities, such as walking or running. The benefits of running for the healing of emotional depression are well-known and recognized. An individual might possess a strong physical learning style or a strong reservoir of mental energy. This kind of person can gain additional nurturance of mind through more mindful interactions with others while engaging in some physical activity for example. Through using some physical energy with one's cognitive self, or the mind's energy, one can then nurture one's emotional side. The same spilling over concept could apply to many other areas of your burgeoning holistic self.

June 28

Trying to follow the way of someone else is often an exercise of frustration. The guidelines for interpersonal wellness involve the focusing of love on one's unique self and creative love. Here is a suggested activity to help you view this principle in action: Try to focus some time thinking within a context, to safely explore your identity. Focus for a moment on what your strengths are; spend five minutes listing positive qualities as you have done before, things liked most and enjoyed about yourself. At the same time, reflect upon an achievement that caused you a positive or proud set of feelings, and why. One of the most difficult aspects of constructively attempting to change is to stay with the process. It is tough to slow down, with this process, and break it into manageable pieces, while reflecting upon it. Try to put time aside to meditate and relax.

Stay with your positive energy.

June 29

The language of feelings and of our spiritual growth is meant to guide and take us into places of higher learning. In these learning places, we improve our psyches, our souls, in order to live and practice mindfulness with others in a more caring way. The language of feelings is the language of emotional evolution. So try to stay with it. Stay in the most loving moments, the still moments of meditative love. Don't get discouraged with things not moving fast enough, just focus on the moment. Do not seek comfort in those temporary relievers of pain, such as alcohol, work, cigarettes, or food. Instead, learn to breathe deeply and naturally. Allow the time to deeply listen to someone. Seek the beauty around you and within you and in the ordinary range of familiar experiences. Reflect upon the wonder of the all that is.

June 30

Go to where the self exists. Self-care is not self-importance, and self caring involves sincerely loving others. Nurturing this authentic self is essential for developing a more emotionally prosperous attitude. It generates more energy to give to others. A loving state is intuitively recognized by the deeper spirit. This more loving, inner self craves growth and development, and authentic give-and-take relationships. Think of some different situations in your life that illustrate this. Perhaps just two or three examples would do. Think of what can be done to improve your life situation using principles of interpersonal wellness. Throughout life, there is a search for meaning that goes on all of the time. We all seek a place of peace and meaning in this world. And often the context we are searching for is within us.

July 1

Specific patterns or blueprints of change are often sought during our lifetime. The answers, if any, are clearest when listening with our inner voice. The deep down feelings, of compassion, love, and the virtue of our connections with others grow best with proper cultivation. Life experiences thrive when the proper conditions for love are fostered.

July 2

Consciously using and applying love in your daily life permits you to notice where the love has already appeared in everyday life. Concentrate on this. Calmly, repeat, gently, with your inner voice, "I will cultivate more love in my life." This natural connection to loving feelings can be adversely affected by a sense of low self-esteem or feelings of meaninglessness in the world. Low self-esteem robs you of an exceptional appreciation of your sense of worth as a loving part of our creative world. Low self-esteem leads the way to minimal self-awareness, and lack of appreciation of others. It is a state of non-love that robs us of our higher consciousness.

July 3

There are many negative consequences of repressing our positive feelings, such as the potential development of disease, process addiction, or painful alienation. Seeking and examining the causes for our low or non-existent self-esteem can be a useful activity for uncovering its roots. In freeing up a positive growth process, we allow for loving roots to grow again, renewed. It can be beneficial and therapeutic to search for innovative and exciting, creative methods of building positive self-esteem.

July 4

Some success-related exercises are helpful in this endeavor and can be implemented simply by spending time doing something that you enjoy doing or that you do well. If an experience you recall from your life felt successful, make a mental note of it. Experience and savor this memory as deeply as you can. This memory can contribute to your current sense of self-esteem. In beginning to build upon this kind of a foundation, you can thus create more situations like this and nurture them.

July 5

There is plenty of literature that deals with the whole area of self-esteem. Browse through a local library or bookstore for some books and this will help activate your process. There are so many it is impossible to list them all and more significantly, one should have the experience of the creative process of looking for something of special interest. As pointed out previously, a major principle of interpersonal wellness is to gain a greater sense of the unique patterns of your more loving self.

July 6

By reading material and paying attention you can significantly assist this process. It is like giving a jump start to any point of your personal growth no matter where you are in the development of interpersonal wellness. It is important to examine, honestly and fully, the reality of your own life and to avoid comparisons with others. The positive activities from every level of your life be they in the physical, emotional, mental or spiritual realm, and your own unique combination of them, is essential in order to get more grounded in this process of interpersonal wellness.

July 7

Staying with the process of creating interpersonal wellness on a daily basis means giving up self-orientation in order to follow a total integration of the more loving self in relation to others.

To know how to mindfully breathe in is to know how to take in and appreciate the full creation of this universe and learn how to love it more. We can do this instinctively; no one has to teach us how to do it. It is a natural part of our self-actualizing nature.

July 8

We need to breathe in order to survive and it is the same with love. Love is the food of our soul, body and psyche. It is energy placed here, for the world, both within and outside of our physical life.

The breath of life is a metaphor for the giving and receiving of the universe's loving energy. Various types of plant growth illustrate this, as they seem to intuitively know of this principle. With every exchange of their energy, they grow, become green, and, in turn, give off more energy. All loving energies of the physical world abide by such harmonies and vibrations of nature. Such intimate exchanges occur within us because of the dramatic exchanges of the environment between and within all people.

July 9

This exchange is unconscious, in that one does not have to consciously think about it. For example, to not consciously think about breathing, yet still breathe the air in and out of the body is miraculous as it sustains the life force. This process defies conscious analysis and yet some kind of thoughtful or mindful energy is causing it to happen. This does not and should not have to feel like a lot of work. The creation of synergistic love is similar. It begins to more unconsciously happen once an initial focus is genuinely made and maintained through nurturing activities.

July 10

Observe a household pet, (say, a dog or a cat), and make a mental note of the kinds of love they practice, and how reactive they are to love's presence in others. Most likely they do this without attributing much conscious thought to it. It is a process of their daily lives. While visiting a zoo, or pet store, you can observe this same phenomenon as pets interact with the loving and concerned humans around them. This sense of healthy, loving energy, this breathing in and out of love, inspires interactions with others.

This loving foundational area is one's spiritual core, connecting deeply to its infinite roots, and with places, signals and beings unseen. This area gives way to our emotional core, a home base to our feeling guides, the overall state of our emotional health or psyche; or it is what works to keep us emotionally connected to our spiritual side. This next layer is the mental, foundational area, or, the mind. It is what works to help us focus, or attain a clear state of our being. All layers are important.

July 11

The least significant piece of who we are in the overall spiritual realm of the world is our physical appearance, our bodily appearance, style of dress, chronological age, hair color, body type, skin color and so on. Because our needs have been structured differently, it is easy to mix up these spiritual components, yet they are all essential in order to adequately practice love focused and emotionally prosperous living. Take a moment, collect a blank sheet of paper, and list the significant areas of yourself. Which areas are strongest for you?

July 12

What areas need work? In what ways can your layers be fortified or strengthened? In this unique form of innermost creativity, this framework can be a helpful tool, an important guide for change. This is another way to view one's process while moving through change and becoming a more love-focused, interpersonally mindful person. At any stage of growth, tools and descriptions are only useful in so far as how we use them. They do not fall neatly into rigid categories or easily predictable processes. For example, the stages of grief that have been developed by Elizabeth Kubler Ross are fairly well known and are meant to be flexible.

Rarely does anyone fall neatly, predictably or rigidly into these categories of grief- shock, anger, denial, depression, bargaining and acceptance. Yet they are so universal that most people can easily relate to them, and identify movement through a grief process.

July 13

In recovering from trauma or from any painful kind of event, it is important to ultimately find, define, and develop one's own way. For example, the following stages can be used to help identify the emotional healing process:

1. Identify what your source of emotional pain is. Move to a place of honest recognition. Begin to genuinely experience feelings around this pain, with as much detail as possible.

2. Pull inward. This is the opposite of isolation. As pain recognition increases, one becomes more authentic and begins elicitation of interpersonal risk. The search for recollections helps to anchor us. Our friends, books we can relate to, counselors, groups, other kinds of support are important. It is okay to need encouragement and move inward, in order to be more honest with yourself and others and seek a greater all-around self and world awareness.

3. Move outward. This process is similar to number two above, but with the energy flowing more naturally outward and with more trust consistently developing in people, places, and things around you.

4. Move beyond feelings. This is essential for staying unstuck; it is the ability to be more fully accepting of one's self's spiritual reality and that of others. The recognition of greater forces in the world allows the psyche to be more genuinely forgiving, more deeply loving, and more serene. There is a forceful recognition of life as a spiritual partnership with others.

July 14

Another part of our growth process is the tolerance for ambiguity. Ambiguity, uncertainty, inconsistency and incongruity all seem to play a major role in the overall plan of the human condition. One might ask how such concepts could be created in a universe that apparently seems blessed with an ample amount of elegance, beauty, symmetry and clarity.

Yet these opposites all form a single, unified whole. We are all one.

July 15

Our universe is dark and light, clear and unclear with qualities and undercurrents that consist of many shades of gray. It is in many ways, like a huge, mystical jigsaw puzzle, with some inter-locking and well matched pieces, and some, not so. How can we learn to handle ambiguity in the midst of pain? Do we accept pieces of our puzzle that do not fit in the usual way? Or, do we discard them? Get angry? Pray? Tolerance for ambiguity is the medicine for the soul when it becomes sick, tired, or too rigid. To embrace ambiguity as a companion in the universe, to make it our friend, teacher, and guide, can be emotionally life-saving as well as spiritually healing. Learning to live our gray areas helps the soul integrate. This love of "all that is" essential to our integrated practice of interpersonal wellness. Interpersonal mindfulness needs to occur in a time frame appropriate for our pure and genuine loving, and for that, the "present" is the best time orientation in which to do our work- in the here and now, each and every day.

July 16

Being here now is more difficult than it at first may seem. It means paying very close attention to the moment, being in the present, fully. It means paying attention to our breathing and fully allowing the self to be whole and listen to others. It means being with the totality of feeling, thinking, and doing. It means a deep understanding and recognition of the fact that this moment is all that we have at any one, given, point in time.

July 17

The basis of many major systems of thought that describe human growth processes and theories of development are present oriented. Without a focus on the moment we cannot really, fully, work on the self. Present oriented living helps one to be more heartfelt, more loved focused, and more truthful with others. There is not always a worry about what to say next, or do, and it means fewer fears about connecting with others in the moment. Being here now, in this moment, is very difficult, but also intensely freeing.

July 18

Take an opportunity to set aside five to ten minutes to be alone today, if possible, or as soon as you can. Try to focus on the present. Try to prevent your thoughts from drifting forward into the future, or backward toward your past. Try this exercise while talking with someone, and really listen to what the other person is saying to you in that moment, right then. Enjoy the feelings of serenity that come with this enjoyment of a shared moment. To enjoy being fully with others in the moment is at the heart of all interpersonal mindfulness.

July 19

To be attuned to each moment and feel more healing, while being grounded and loving toward others is to become more in tuned with your own inner self. Our inner clocks or unseen emotional time sensors run on distinct cycles, different time measures from our outside physical clocks. This interior world of feeling time can sometimes seem quite slow, as if it runs according its own processes. At times emotional time can be experienced as moving through quantum leaps. Emotional time, with its own growth process, respects our emotional choices, yet can be affected by our emotional resistance as well. Emotional time is, at times, fueled by defense mechanisms or by our systems of blocks, although on the surface it may not seem so. All is not as it seems in the world of the psyche.

July 20

Experiencing life knowing of this emotional way is not easy and more of a risk, but eventually, the way toward growth. Inevitably, we run out of excuses not to experience this. To begin the release of our deeper, innermost and powerful dynamics makes way for more love focused living, and more interpersonal wellness in our lives. The dynamics in our soul's world speak with the language of feelings, with external physical facts of reality less predominant. Our innermost messages follow the flow of where love-focused feelings and interpersonal mindfulness adeptly coexist.

July 21

While at the ocean, or by any body of water, gently watch the water. Carefully observe the changes that have taken place in and around the water. If it is the ocean, watch the ebb and flow of its waves: Observe the kinds of changes that have taken place in the sand, stones, trees, and plants all around. Major changes have occurred over time to this boundary area of where ocean meets land. The changes have occurred in infinitesimal steps and stages over time, significant yet barely discernible at any one time. Doesn't this beautiful world of nature have something to teach our world of feelings? Is it sharing messages of important processes, for our inner, deeper worlds of psychic change?

July 22

This ebb and flow builds beauty, change and love in the world, but not without dangers and risks. Nature speaks to us in many ways. There are myriad changes that occur naturally and ones that we humans create artificially. These dangers frequently block the creation of emotionally prosperous living. Another's likes, dislikes, or behaviors do not have to be unconditionally accepted, especially if they are harmful. Someone else's inner self or presence is working itself out in this universe and experiencing its own lessons. Spiritual growth is a uniquely private thing and not ours to judge.

July 23

Walk in the woods or anywhere outdoors. This is a wonderful ways to seek the comfort of nature, with peace, tranquility and spiritual dynamism. This is how spirit can know and lead you as you walk. One's inner self knows how to move toward a more loving place, seek loving guidance, and not give in to or accept harsh or painful judgment. When left free of clutter and given a loving setting, the spirit soars.

July 24

The skills of centering, focusing, and relaxing all can be practiced independently. They are most helpful to the practice of loving detachment and interpersonal wellness. An important principle of interpersonal growth is that we become healthier with a sense of consciously, deeply loving others' spirits, loving one's neighbor as well as the natural wonders all around us. These are examples of the difference between selfishness and self caring activities. It is important to have a loving compassion for one's own psyche as well as for the creation of more loving energies for our world. Without this, the dynamics of acceptance, forgiveness, gratitude, and healthy relationships would not be possible.

July 25

Healthy connections depend upon a consciousness of sanctity and appealing to the divine nature of all human encounters. Foundations of healthy connections are comfortable and centered. Take time to look at this overall scheme of growth and development in the world. Ask who you are, and equally importantly, who you are not. Know of your limitations on this earth. Know that any one person cannot be in charge of all that is. Each of us is only in charge of our self, and of loving others whom we encounter.

July 26

Loving in this manner involves the close examination of intimacy, and knowing that divine interpersonal intimacy is different from sexuality. We don't learn this naturally, or easily, nor is it simple to keep in mind, yet it is possible to become more accustomed to sensing this sacred emotional closeness with one another.

July 27

Given our overpopulated world, we do not have any trouble with sexuality. But we do, given our needless interpersonal violence, hate crimes and judgments have a lot of difficulty with intimacy. We do not, as yet, experience the ever-present and universal, energy of love in this world, nor do we share it deeply with our family members, friendships, or co-workers. It is blocked as we run form it in daily life, all around the world.

July 28

Growing into a place of this kind of intimacy is scary yet nurturing. It is what will lead us to another place, an evolutionary state of loving. This is scary because we have learned no clear rules about this. Yet we are obviously in a spiritual crisis. There is a need to reclaim humanity's collective loving energy, even if it means that to love we must risk, and it is not too late. It is never too late to give this a good, honest try. It may mean there will be more floundering and some pain. But our reward will be well worth the price of trying.

Let no one be spiritually rejected in your life today or in your days hereafter. Give to others the love and knowledge of love and intimacy that you have deep inside you. Continue to go about your life's business, but go in a more consciously mindful and loving way.

July 29

To attain this more relaxed, gentle and love focused state, means to naturally rid the self's unnecessary tensions, and increase explicitly positive feelings about the psyche and of others' psyches. The psyche's positive experiences will teach more awareness of countless deeper and clearer spiritual messages about many aspects of your life. As feelings of gentle relaxation engage you, there will be more kindness with the self's spirit and hence more kindheartedness with others.

July 30

Feelings of life esteem will gradually and gently increase. Others in your life naturally will be held in higher esteem. A realization of others and the world in a special and unique way will become more evident. A positive, authentic, inner self will emerge and naturally achieve more of its potential. This process will become more natural as it takes root, grows and helps to find the center of your soul, as you learn to settle down and get close to your innermost authenticity.

July 31

Our innate, physical comfort exists naturally with our spiritual comfort. By allowing our relaxing energy to sink in deeply, our breathing continually energizes the soul. Focusing more on love in our world, the love in our lives, and love in the moment, means to let the entire body feel this natural sensation, with no distractions, no negative self-talk. It means to allow the complete bliss of gentleness and loving feelings to flow through you.

August 1

In life, we often hear a lot about certain diagnoses, failed relationships, and so on, that determine our psychological health or the lack thereof. This kind of framework can be helpful at times, but also easy to feel overwhelmed with what is wrong with us. This may occur to you even as you read through this book. It is important to remember that positive growth happens in many different ways. It is essential to accept ambiguity of chaotic change and the basic nature of the world. Do not try and control it.

August 2

It is important to not compare yourself with anyone else, and realize that deep down, we are each so different from one another. We are each as weak or strong, emotionally, as anyone else. We each have different patterns. You are all right just the way you are -whole, perfect, loving, and lovable. Change must come from within you not from anyone else. Ultimately the inner self is the judge of what is chosen for the profound changes.

August 3

Write down your own stages of healing that you recognize. Write of any distinct progress made in each of your areas. Notice, with this exercise, that there are at times when patterns are evident. In each of us, there are extremes of the soul, from being accepting, to being hard on ourselves or others, from judging, to sharing openly and positively with one another; from easily believing, to quickly doubting. Most of us are in between these extremes on any given day. And no one is perfect.

August 4

Life is a process of ongoing work. We are each a unique combination, a special mosaic of the soul's being in the world. By understanding and respecting this uniqueness we travel into the deepest parts of the psyche. In taking this journey of the psyche, we are led to a greater level of knowledge, and a greater level of acceptance of the all that is. Our journey is capable of bringing joy into life along with an acknowledgment of its deeper meaning. It is a journey we would have never thought possible. Yet, interpersonal wellness allows us to have a more tuned in life of understanding and potentiality, to feel much better. This loving effect, this centering effect, is where "what is" merges with "what is possible."

August 5

Make two columns on a sheet of paper and list "what is" on one side, and "what is possible" on the other. Compare your lists and find one thing to try in the near future and to make a commitment of achieving. Know that you are capable of this change as you ponder the following meditation:

Imagine walking on level ground. This, you could call routine, or mundane living. Imagine coming upon a hole that looks like a very deep well. Look inside of it. Although the bottom is not visible, you sense that a part of the self in there is strong. Keep looking in and be drawn more towards it. On certain days, you could ignore it, but in looking today around at all the trees and grass, the sky, the plants in the nearby fields, you sense that the hole as well is part of all that is. It takes more energy in fact, to ignore the depth of the hole than to acknowledge it and look down, squarely. The initial assessment of the potential work needed in order to go down may be in knowing exactly how deep the hole is, or in knowing how dark and how cold it is down there. It is lonely; there is the potential of being stuck or left down there to die. This is a primal fear, metaphorically. It is horrifying to think about being so alone, so abandoned, so scared.

Yet there is hope.

August 6

Suddenly, as you visualize further, the hole, like a steep mountain clearly has sides, potential steps, and places to hold and behold and be one with the earth. Places upon which to climb upward toward the light. Suddenly the hole appears to be very different; its darkness actually a teacher, a guide. As a theater for the soul to search through from the perspective of looking down, the hole seems as if one could be engulfed and swallowed up. But from the perspective of looking up, while one climbs the mountain toward daylight, all is not as it seemed.

August 7

It is likely possible, in the near future, to encounter such a hill to climb, to walk on its two sides from this perspective. Like the hole, it is all a matter of perception. The side of any mountain may in fact be the wall of a cave or well. The key to our inner learning is to avoid the complacent level ground for it is while we are on the plateau.

August 8

Learning to love at the deepest levels means visualizing one's self as a healthy and loving being, prosperously living on a robust, kind and connected earth, with sound interpersonal ethics guiding all of our interpersonal relationships.

August 9

Panhuman loving is the deepest loving of all within humanity as it is the bigger picture of who we are, of our existence on this earth. This larger picture is now emerging for more of us to see, as the sum total of many of our individual journeys on many different levels that occur daily. For many of us on these journeys, the final outcome is love; it is our primary, driving force.

August 10

Constantly creating and recreating our individual potential and jointly co-creating a deeper, authentic, nature of humanity does depend upon the awareness and removals of all hatred and violence.

A newer, more refreshing priority is currently being placed upon constructs and ways of loving, such as acceptance, forgiveness, spiritual values, a feeling awareness, and more authentic closeness with others. We are, each of us, individually, like lightning sparks that can create more spiritual, creative energy, leading to an interpersonal reawakening of growth and development.

August 11

With our initial seeds, comes the commitment of the level of loving responsibility toward oneself and others. Without this level of responsibility, we could not fully be there for our earth and its life consciousness. Without a higher feeling for oneself, we cannot truly love, authentically love, our neighbors, family and friends. This is why it can be so healing to share feelings, to elicit and nurture trust, intuition, and use our positive instincts and inclinations. This leads us to be more aware of the overall value of the human psyche itself.

August 12

As one shares more of the self, it becomes something that is more valued. The more loving qualities of energy in life emerge, even in simple things. One can see this, even in examining flowers, pictures, books, the people who walk past you, or in something more complex, such as intuitive relationships with others. The beauty is hard to miss.

August 13

Several psychotherapy theories have become very popular. This may be a sign that there has been not only a lot of interest but also a tremendous amount of positive, empowering psychological progress made by many individuals, and our society at large. But much more potential is evident. As with any sudden growth or movement forward, there remains the potential for misunderstanding or misdirection. Self-growth does not mean growth of an "I" at the expense of the nurturance of interdependent relationships and human communities. We are all creatures of this world, citizens of the universe.

August 14

No one person is better than anyone else. If we unfairly label or criticism others, or engage in any cruel judgment of others, then the potential for evil lurks closely behind. Criticism drains the spirit and negatively affects positive connections with others.

August 15

One is, as an individual, capable and responsible of growing spiritually and lovingly, and to individuate in one's own loving way, to become what one is capable of becoming. Judgmental behaviors run the risk of alienation and prejudice, and often are enemies of the soul, diseases of the psyche. The questions: Where do I belong? How do I live? Have I unintentionally alienated myself from others? Do I judge others for who they are? Do I create unnecessary walls of separation between myself and others?

August 16

Perhaps there is a dormant part of the self that has some underlying important and hidden meaning, just waiting to help integrate all of our more loving parts. Sometimes, unnecessary fear and paranoia can potentially block the way of this authentic, special part of the self, and cause it to carry additional, uncalled-for, defensiveness and useless energy at our interpersonal expense. Is there such a place within you that is dormant? Is it hidden out of fear? We all share a common language of defensiveness, often masking the deeper, more loving self.

August 17

What does it mean to you to be protective of your most inner self? How can you learn to access more of it? Instinctively, we know when we are near an inner place of deep solace, comfort and truth. This calm spreads throughout the whole being. This foundation of tranquility gives us the energy to carry ourselves into a more advanced level of awareness.

August 18

The inner landscape is rich with meaning. Draw upon it frequently, and move inwardly, toward the self. Allow the landscape to be nurtured further. Realize that there is a choice and that no matter what you are you are a person worthy of love, respect, and spiritual fulfillment. The nature of your inner light and its reflection within the whole universe can elicit many loving feelings. Reflect upon what we humans are made of; what kinds of elements do you see in the eyes of others? What are your thoughts when you observe a picture of the brain? How do you react to the miracle of life?

August 19

The human brain is an organism that is capable of reflecting upon itself and may even be capable of connecting us into another dimension. Our brain, like a hidden observer could be running a video camera in this three-dimensional world that we live in so that our thoughts, feelings, perceptions, are all markers for a world of some distant, soul-related dimension that is also ours - our higher self, peacefully working on itself and learning from our various explorations.

August 20

Before we are able to change our deeper and more loving self or move into our psychic structure, we have to learn how to observe ourselves in action. This can be learned in individual psychotherapy or in a group, but we must at first learn to live kind of on "two tracks"- to be thinking about thinking, or having an awareness for feelings and others' feelings or, in general, creating in a sense, another level of consciousness that runs parallel to what we perceive in the here and now.

August 21

It is within the birth of many of these new, parallel sorts of consciousness that the hope of our species lies. Take some time now for yourself to acknowledge your inner observer. Take some time to acknowledge a higher self, God, nature, your Creator, the unconscious, the collective nature of your surrounding energy or whatever framework you choose. Consciously, give out thanks for the strength, discipline and determination that operates in the all that is, in our physical and spiritual world. And thank the many observers for the giving of such ability. Notice how good it feels as you learn to do this.

August 22

A higher quality and everlasting sense of intimacy with others, goes far beyond familial or fundamental blood ties. Human blood, or, that which is in each and every one of us, comes ultimately from the same place. It is the realization of an essence of this deeper truth, which teaches us that we must all be connected. It is as if, as we approach the future, we are sneaking a peek over a cliff. And, while it might in some ways be scary, this view leads us to the gradual uncovering of the layers of the reality of our existence. Consciousness, as it peels off its many layers, finds the numerous connections that exist in our collective mind.

August 23

The conscious human mind is undergoing an evolutionary leap of consciousness of dynamic proportions. We are coming out of a fog and need to realize that we are all connected. If we are going to survive, and go beyond simple clinging to life, then we need to become better at it, to arrive on the other side of where we are now. In life, we have no doubt undergone many changes, each of which is usually a step closer towards one's truths. To peel back layers, than can each be explored at any given time is not impossible. Inner truth is a gradual process, and it is a healing process, whether done alone, with another friend, or with a group of others.

August 24

The human energy struggle is to try and better understand our outside world. There is much sanctity, mystery, fascination and satisfaction involved in all of this explanation. Our physical senses have worked, throughout the centuries, to tune more into this outside world. They, our senses, have even extended themselves, thus attempting to make "human like" extensions capable of searching even further into space, and struggle even more to find clear answers, clearer meanings. To seek out those places, or those answers, which would give us some indication, or some guide as to our meaning in this vast and wondrous universe is a central guiding force of our lives.

August 25

The key point here is that this universe consists of more than what we have access to with our physical senses. Our senses are only one type of exploration, in a limited spectrum of space time. For example, vision, is both an inner and outer vision. And what of hearing? A sense of touch? Smell? What of memories of senses? If a human sense is lost, or if one never had a certain sense or senses, how does one compensate or maximize the utilization of others? How does one know what isn't there? How does one utilize other senses? As you reflect upon these qualities, the reality of our "inner" senses becomes more evident.

August 26

There are greater levels of hidden and inner potentials within each of us. There are great, underlying collective meanings in life; and this is often not very obvious to us throughout most of life. The potential is there, lying in a mostly undiscovered state. It is yet very exciting to become more tuned into this state, into this potential, and to see what lies there. Often this is the essence of the road toward becoming more of who you are. By tuning in, which is itself a challenging and painful event, we must remove our masks and our emotional protections. During our youth, we have often learned to utilize such masks, in order to protect our deepest and inner most pain.

August 27

With time, especially as we move into adulthood, we may learn to overuse our defenses. If defenses are overused this in turn may lead us into a state of total shielding. They can deprive us of genuine joy in life. A life of greater meaning and intensity means connecting to an advanced level of collective love, and passion for the greater good. This is the actuality of intimacy without a mask, the kind we most often crave, an intimacy with others, with God, and with our own psyche.

August 28

Just for today, for this one point in time, we can listen to this inner peacefulness. Then we can move toward the practice of this for each and every day. Try to capture the many rhythms of this actuality and try to hear its inner flow. Hear it as a major focal point of the natural order of things. The currents of this inner flow involve many aspects of love, giving it, and receiving it. Cultivate the love that lies inside of this energy, today and always in your life.

August 29

While ushering in our new era, this new evolution of consciousness, we need to emphasize being, and not doing so much in an unbalanced state. One has to fight off a lot of the old conditioning in order to find the truth of the inner self. Thinking more lovingly builds essence and essence is the focal point of the inner self. Unfortunately, there is more language for the phenomena that occur outside of us than for the inner spaces of the psyche. There is no quick or magical component that will usher us into this new era, no esoteric inner pathway that needs to be discovered. With focused work, one becomes more a true inner self.

August 30

Many of us who wish for a "blueprint," soon recognize that there is no standard or easy way to do this. We may use guidelines as tools, by we each must find our own, individual, unique way. Like the unending process of self actualization, each of our journeys has a beginning and yet no end. Each sojourn is a highly personal and unique pattern, known deeply, in a spiritual way, to each one of us.

August 31

Each person's pattern has a special and unique character of loving potentiality, one that cannot be quantified or compared, it can only become. One must suffer, however, in some respect, in order to learn of the great truths in life, and about oneself. Otherwise there is no meaning, no life, and no journey of learning, only a shallow shadow of meaning, barely reflective of one's self.

September 1

Enhancement of the inner life, through prayer, meditation, or by the creation of meaningful and mindful personal contacts, allows for the development of a greater meaning in this universe, and this thus has a positive effect on our outside interactions. The reverse is only a delusion, because material riches and other tangible things simply do not last. The truth is in the land of the soul, the spirit, and in the collective, loving consciousness around us.

September 2

By focusing on the creative visualization of love, we enhance the spirit. Imagine a more loving world. See the transcending of our basic, animal natures, transform into our divine birthright, our real selves, as we continue to live on this earth. We must search for our true meaning in this world, and give conscious thought to love focused realities and develop related belief systems and values more in line with this. Otherwise, there is a lack of completeness, a sense that our most important journey cannot move forward.

September 3

Enhancing the vantage point of the psyche means to create more love.

What of our so-called negative feelings? Disappointment? Irritation? Anger? Is anger ever appropriate? When is it inappropriate? When is expressing a true and genuine catharsis to heal the spirit an addictive or nonproductive rage? Our more primal, innate anger may no longer be appropriate for human beings as a species. We have evolved beyond this, conquered the world it seems in ways we may have needed to in order to survive, engaged in wars, and plundered our earth long enough.

September 4

We no longer need to pursue the territorialism that has so characterized our species for so long. We are becoming another species, guided by our mindful and loving nature. What good does anger do that leads us to physical violence? What good are we if we succeed in destroying ourselves? Yet, anger related to the desire for intimacy or more mindful and authentic interconnection may be more appropriate as we evolve.

September 5

The destruction of our earth is no spiritual catharsis. We need to evolve fully and become more civilized and well integrated. We need to become more appropriately expressive, of not only our anger, but of other feelings as well, and utilize these feelings for what they are, as guides for the spirit. This process begins on an individual level. The effective expression of anger and other feelings involves using proper tools of effective communication. Anger is a pure feeling, and as such should be paid close attention to. Yet it is a unique feeling, unlike no others, because of its power to hurt others.

September 6

There is a greater sense of responsibility needed for the expression of anger, and this involves more levels of hard and mindful work. We need to be aware of it (anger), at first, and next, identify its specific focus, and then express it to ourselves, or within ourselves (or to God, or in a safe place), and then express it outward appropriately; if need be, this could be to another human being, in a manner more befitting to our level of evolution as a species. We are no longer savages. And our feelings are not garbage; to be dumped at will, from one receptacle of human being to the next. Feelings are not meant to be discarded in a destructive manner and then forgotten.

September 7

We should learn from our feelings at all times. We must honor them, all feelings, within ourselves, in our interactions with others, and then utilize them so that our work in this new context of evolution helps us to move forward, with constructive conflict resolution. Feelings should become our major tools for a divinely inspired and more enhanced sense of intimacy with others.

September 8

Being direct with someone else can create a constructive and healing kind of situation as well as help us to build up a solid set of communication skills. Seemingly negative feelings on the surface, such as resentment, irritation, or anger, may actually be some version of hurt or fear, or perceived feelings of a loss of love or interpersonal meaning. These are feelings that can come out rather indirectly more than directly.

September 9

Each of our feelings needs to be acknowledged directly and honestly for what they are. We are not alone on this earth, or in this universe.

We are traveling along with many others, yet we may often feel lonely. Although we are each born and die within a unique space and time, we are, with these many others, sharing a deep human condition. This earth is our collective cradle, our carrier, our ship. Our journey may feel difficult or frustrating, as if we are going nowhere, but one thing seems clear. This is no accident.

September 10

We came from somewhere directly, and we are going somewhere directly. Random chance events could not have created such a sense of order and purpose to life in this world. Someone or something hears, someone likely sees, each and every move we make. And, for sure, we are all in this together. When we might be feeling especially frustrated or unappreciated, it would be worth it to remember the deeper meaning of our feeling-related work, our specific roles in this life, in our family lives, and in our various relationships.

September 11

It would be crucial to begin by reflecting upon the amount of this kind of work you have done in this life already; for to be alive, in many ways, is to struggle and do this work. Most of all look around you. The spirit is not alone. Think of how you create positive moments in your life and try to be encouraging of yourself and your spirit as you gently move your process along. This true, especially with the memories of this day, etched upon our souls forever. It is the gift of one another that carries us through.

September 12

Interpersonal wellness is the consistent recognition of loving connection. Expressions of love are not only reserved for special occasions or holidays, such as Christmas, church masses, hospital visits, or funerals. Interpersonal wellness means the development of positive, loving and nonjudgmental feelings, an around-the-clock feeling of spirituality in relation.

September 13

Interpersonal wellness means to generate and grow the deepest states of good will toward others on one's most spiritual levels. Interpersonal wellness as the foundation of connective happiness means working to create more healthful and healing feelings with an ever-present focus on love.

September 14

With patient steps, and by deeply examining our emotional patterns, we learn what a painful and deliberate process altering our emotional life can be. And it hurts a lot before it feels better, just as in any other growth process. There is a careful examination however, that is drastically needed, before we can fully change some of what we may not like about ourselves or our self-defeating behaviors.

September 15

To be truly effective, this process will take some time. It is often best if done with another trusted person, or in a trusted group of others, or, in the company of what we perceive God to be, or, in a self-help meeting, meditation group, or some other kind of sacred space. The important thing is to be patient and gentle with yourself. Most of our patterns have taken years to form and they do not go away quickly.

September 16

The patterns cannot change overnight. So find the time to discover what works best for you. Then, just do it. Take note, that, for anything truly meaningful in life, there are not "quick fixes", no easy answers, not in our close relationships, not in the counseling process, and not in nature, overall. Lasting and meaningful changes, life's rewards, and close relationships come with time, and with occasional pain as our teacher and guide.

September 17

Just as the earth's oceans take their time to sculpt patterns along the shorelines of the world, it takes time to sculpt the pathways representing our work on the emotional self. This is hard work in order for meaningful change to occur. Observe the gift of now, the best element we have in order to make major changes. "Now" is a concept, a gift continually given to us. It is, in many ways, like being given a blackboard to write on, to erase and try again and again. The universe is a patient place. We don't have to be perfect, not even the second time we try, and on many things we learn best from our mistakes. Mistakes are a central part of our being here, our spiritual lessons. If not, then there would be no blackboard or the spiritual reality of "now."

September 18

In taking the time to study our individual emotional ebbs and tide of emotional growth, we can watch the natural flows of the earth, the ebbs and tides of water, tides, the wind, the sun, the moon and the constellations above us. The hint from nature seems to be surrounding us everywhere: One may need to move forward, backward, reflect, retreat, and make some errors. It is how we best learn, how the world operates. Mistakes are a major part of the plan.

September 19

Perfectionism has no therapeutic or positive purpose.

Recall the times that you attempted to be perfect and how that may have in fact interfered with your personal growth! So create a place for your special work but remember to allow for mistakes. Include meditation, prayer, reflection, time outdoors, fun activities, and be sure they are all easily accessible. One has the right to responsibly create an individual, workable and realistic program of growth. Allow yourself the breathing in time of love focused and positively mindful energy.

September 20

Stressors of a certain type can affect your emotions adversely. They often build up unknowingly and imperceptibly. One day, we might suddenly become aware of a certain stress that has built-up out of control. We need to try and "catch" these built up levels before they peak. Residual stress keeps us out of touch with our innermost feelings. Suddenly, if we find ourselves reacting, or overreacting, to other people, places, things, it is worth examining ourselves at that point, to intercept the accumulated stress.

September 21

Yet much of stress is normal, and without it, we could not function. But recurrent stress with accompanying periodic maintenance helps us with our inner housecleaning, and getting rid of the useless kinds of stress or any unhealthy build-up. Do not judge yourself for this built up stress. It is a normal part of life. Just do something to alleviate it. Take a walk, a short break, go outdoors, or do something peaceful during your lunch hour; spend some moments with reflective silence or just some time alone.

September 22

Focus on the enhanced state of relaxation of your body, do some stretching exercises, buy a new stress management book or tape, or, get a massage. Acknowledge that the strains of life, especially in certain cultures can create a crisis that transforms into an opportunity, and that can, symbolically and metaphorically, become the same thing. Think back on your own history, on the so-called crisis points of your life. Chances are the crises presented opportunities as well.

September 23

The metaphor appears constantly before us in nature: an earthquake destroys, and then causes rebuilding. A death causes loss, then rebirthing. A storm destroys, yet it clears the air. Likewise, the ending of a relationship often causes a new beginning in one's life. Graduations are terminations yet they are also often the beginnings of new experiences.

September 24

Change hurts us often yet it opens up the gate for new ventures and adventures, again and again, throughout the cycles of nature and in our lives.

Notice how changes occur within the world around you. Notice how the weather, the trees, the structure of a town or city forms patterns. Think of the crucial relationships in your life and their history and meaning. Is there a perceivable pattern? Has crisis ever meant an opportunity in relationships? What has been in this relationship of change? To a large degree, all of life involves change. It is everywhere: in nature, within us, in our dreams, outside of the earth's solar system indeed, within our entire universe. How does, or has, change worked in life, on a more personal level? How is this process of change most effective-through prayer, other people, from within you, or from your own thoughts? Or, is it all of these, or some combination of them to some degree?

September 25

Are there most effective ways to change? It is compelling to think that within each of us, change occurs through some combination of thoughts, feelings, behaviors, and that we each form our own, unique pattern of change specific to the essence of who we are.

While describing or writing out a plan for change, while recognizing that you possess a unique pattern of constructive change within yourself, it must also be reasonable. In what ways do changes work best for you? What steps can be taken and trusted, such as intuition, drive, a love of work, or a new focus on others? There are powerful hints in the pattern of one's life for making positive changes. Changing on an emotional level is an important activity and we often need to renew the practice daily.

September 26

Often people can be important catalysts for change yet, if we listen carefully enough, there are other hints, guides, directions for change present around us, and accessible in life.

This does not mean having to avoid giving and receiving corrective or constructive feedback. Often the most positive or most constructive elements of life are the hardest to hear, and are the most obviously present. Think of a meaningful compliment you recently received, as an example.

September 27

When thinking back, what made this kind of a compliment meaningful? What made it have an impact upon you? Does this kind of a process provide any hints for you about how to build upon some of your unique strengths? Allow your source of strength to grow deep in the roots of your authentic being. Acceptance of one's self is the essential positive point for beginning to build one's sense of spiritual self-esteem. Begin with your strengths, and gradually work from there. Gradually build an emotionally prosperous home with a tough foundation.

September 28

Finding our spiritual home or that place deep inside of us, where the deepest self and one's deepest feelings are accepted obviously connects to the higher purposes of the universe. Often a spiritual pathway is filled with pain, hardships and risks of one form or another. But as our search continues, and is eventually found, and we gradually familiarize the self with a deeper self, and gradually discover the true, inner "higher beliefs" of our reality, they will become pathways filled with more joy, self-awareness and more positive relationships, and continued growth on many levels. Recognition of our true strengths is often difficult and long process, more arduous than in determining your weaknesses.

September 29

It is rather involved to find a center, a focal point, from which to work.

Try to look at yourself as a whole or total person, and list strengths in each area of this whole. This unfolding of your overall strengths, as a complete person, is an excellent place from which to begin this focal kind of work. The long and slow pathway of getting to know the self, better and better, and coming to terms with it and with what needs to change, are at the core of anyone's spiritual journeying.

September 30

Spirituality, and seeking deeper meaning of life, and discovering our creativity all provide a greater sense of feelings awareness with patience, better tolerance for ambiguity, and a true desire to harm no one along the way. Growth obtained at the expense of someone else, creates an additional backlog of spiritual garbage, and the metaphorical stench from this garbage will eventually get you, even if for a while; it never goes undiscovered.

October 1

Remember that your spirit is not alone. At times it may seem so, or in the other extreme, it may seem like a crowded journey. One must always, respectfully, make room for others. Honor all psyches in their places of growth. Search all around in the interpersonal energy fields in your midst, and gauge the pathways of prosperity around you. When seeking others, or having needs, do so respectfully while experiencing these new feelings, remember to respect the golden rule of emotional growth, and bring harm to no one, including yourself.

October 2

Authentically connecting with others is one of the most gratifying, energizing, and hopeful elements there is in the world. This factor is still an unrealized and untapped energy source in many of our relationships. Authentic or real connections with another, are often synergistic, and can build further connection of phenomenal potential and interactive power. Identification of daily gratitude in relation to others will cause this potential and power to increase.

October 3

It is time for taking some giant steps in our journey toward intimacy. Working on having better communication skills can go a long way in life. Communication skills, especially verbal and nonverbal forms of communication, are the major tools we have for effectively connecting with others. We are not evolved enough yet, or quite intuitive enough, to really guess or know what is going on in the mind of another person, no matter how close we may be to another or how well we may know him or her.

October 4

Yet, working on verbal communication especially can yield tremendous results, even if it is long, tiring, and tedious work. This may seem exhausting sometimes to, for example break communication down into tiny, seemingly minuscule pieces of understanding; but often, this is the primary way to handle it. There is no realistic, long lasting short cut. We would never think that in order to become a marathon runner (or even a fairly good runner) we would be engaging in a quick and easy process either.

October 5

The same rule of no short cuts applies to becoming a more effective communicator, a more effectively loving human being.

To make a better effort at utilizing good communication skills we might begin in the following manner:

To listen, to really deeply listen, to others.

· To not try to make any assumptions; check things out.

To use some basic assertiveness, "I messages." Own things clearly, and take responsibility for what you are communicating.

Share your affection more freely, give compliments and point out positive feelings toward others.

October 6

To be here now, and accept this kind of a working journey, means also that small, interpersonal miracles begin to happen. Cultivate a sense of openness, acceptance, and compassion in your daily life. Realize the extent that life itself is no chance happening, for the creation or any one of us here is a miracle! Good things happen, often with pain, but often in a peaceful pattern of learning as well. Everyone here is simultaneously a teacher and learner for one another. Everyone needs relationships as spiritual tools for they are the spiritual essence of the breathing life force.

October 7

Feel the intense passion of communication going on, as a flow of a creative, positive power put in the hearts of every man and woman around you. Find and spend some time with a flowing river, an ocean or clouds, as they move about briskly about in the sky. Watch the birds in fervent flight, just as a breathing, active group of human beings. Communication is an ever-present force around us.

October 8

Who set all of this in motion? Who creates it? Who moves it? How do you express love toward these forces? Trusting in the higher good is a basic principle of interpersonal mindfulness that requires vigilant patience. Experiencing labor pain comes not only with childbirth. There is a continuous birthing process that occurs in our lives, if we allow it to, every day.

October 9

There are many principles, just as in childbirth, of how this growth and change process works in daily life. They form the core of our human experience, on deep, emotional levels. In order to achieve a pathway of potential, through the spirit, requires the knowledge that a mysterious, mapping force, comes with our emotional patterns as much as within physical life, something like DNA. In formulating our gathering of a nutritional spiritual growth force via letting our more loving nature to happen, we grow more into a safe place for the psyche, and we are, at times, heard by others on a similar pathway.

October 10

Planning our specific journey is a lot like moving through a dark tunnel, at times, or through a cave, towards the light. Going through life's struggles and pains, and allowing our unconscious to do its work, ultimately, helps us to achieve better contact with others; prepares us to give love, and receive love in a more meaningful way and truly connect. Birthing emotionally is an essential part of our human story.

October 11

How did our birth occur? What was the event of our physical birth like? How did, or do, other people around you describe it? What implications does this have for your psychic journey, right now in life? The relationship of sexuality and intimacy is another powerful area to explore. Patterns of intimacy are markers for how we get closer to others. It should not be a power struggle, or battle of opposites, nor an objectification or platform from which to show off skills and techniques of closeness. If we fall prey to any of these arenas, then we are not truly with, or in synch with another, but we are engaging in a one-person drama, hoping to get our one-way needs met.

October 12

What can be done with our intimate, close, nonsexual relationships can often help us to learn about this flowing with another concept, a lot better. From those people in your life that you care a lot about, but whom you are nonsexual with, you can learn a lot. Of these people, pick at least one or two with whom you would like to be closer. Ask yourself if there is one thing that could be done with, or for, each person in order to have a more healthy relationship or one that flows better. Then, in the next week, observe any dynamic or major changes that may result.

October 13

Initiate spending more quality time with this person, share an experience, or, directly share some authentic feelings.

Deep inside each of us is the capacity for more intimate love. It is music for our souls-a composition of passion, joys and many peak experiences. Some of this is sad, while other elements of it are rites of passage, or others meant to be humorous. Some aspects of it may even ease the pain within us.

October 14

The full range of feelings often acts as a symphony orchestra conductor for our human experiences, as we listen carefully and watch. We gradually become more capable of tuning in better and playing. By such progressively fine tuning, our listening and observing skills transform into energies that we can use and that we never realized we had.

October 15

Begin each moment with a deep breath, a positive thought and an appreciation for all that you have learned from others in this life. What you have learned in relation likely surpasses any kind of memorization or book learning you have thus far received. When framed within a meaningful relationship, knowledge has renewed power and application.

October 16

Listen to some music that brings you feelings of love. Listen to the inner love happening within you. Even five minutes of this can go a long way in order to nurture your soul. Hear your spirit; and then, fine tune it.

There are many kinds of love in our world. It is a novel and strange concept to dislike or judge any kind of loving! This contradiction escapes many, for the fear that ensues and builds eventually into hatred, is reminiscent of the way that prejudice builds into evil.

October 17

It must be, on some level, insecurity about what love means, what intimacy means, or what sexuality, as a total experience, means. Because of our early and ongoing ignorance as a species, we often cannot separate sexuality from intimacy, nor can we separate either of them from the biological concept of reproduction. In spite of the fact that we need reproduction less and less in our world, and actually need pure love more, we both hate and fear, a concept that purports to do both.

October 18

The terrors and the prejudices of the psyche are strange indeed. Often they need the capacity to safely talk, connect, dialogue, share, and breathe out their tensions and fears, in order to give the mind a chance to work more properly and discover its inconsistencies. There is still much hope for the many kinds of expressions of non-harmful and nonviolent love in this world.

October 19

There are many ways to express and learn about closeness, warmth and sexuality in terms of non-reproductive intimacy. What images are conjured up in your mind about love or, about platonic relationships between two adults? Very close friendships? Are there any fears or insecurities that you can identify within yourself? If so, what is the focus of them? How do any of these connect with your views of the world, your own biology, evolution, or where you believe we are going as a species? How do they relate to your system of spirituality?

October 20

What does normal mean to you? What constitutes a close, or an intimate relationship? Is there room in this world, do you think, for more loving and safe, mutual expressions of caring between two unrelated adults? A life out of context from the meaning of others is not a real, vital, or connected life. Meaningful relationships with others often lead to more genuineness and authenticity, which in turn, can heal other aspects of the self and the cycle, continues onward toward a more healthful, growth producing way of life. Isolated self growth blocks this important and vital energy we receive when connecting with others.

October 21

Obviously there is a lot to think about in these realms. There is a lot involved in exploring, as individuals, what it means for us as human beings to be more attached. Yet, this is perhaps what we each want, more than anything. There are many rules about relating, in our culture, and their origins are important to discover in whatever type of social structure that you inhabit.

October 22

One important aspect of all of this is to look at how the existence of loving energy works when it is active in this world. Should it ever be limited, do you think, and if so, why? What is the relationship of the repression of intimacy to the growth of hatred or of negative feelings in the world?

October 23

With the probable arrival of yet another wave of a more intensified and holistic human potential movement in our new millennium, we have to be careful that, as a species, we are not setting ourselves up to fail or to become too narcissistic. We cannot place unrealistic ideals upon ourselves, or ones that are impossible to achieve; yet, we should not sell ourselves short either, or ignore our incredible level of potential heretofore untapped to a large degree. Our goals, when clear and achievable, can be attained.

October 24

The principles of love focused, emotionally prosperous living strive to meet this balance between realism and our potential. With lofty and idealistic goals, or by placing too many demands upon our psyche, we can make changes or concrete progress extremely difficult.

October 25

Self-centeredness takes a phenomenal amount of work, whereas interpersonal wellness creates additional energy and a greater feeling of manageability around our own life's goals. By cultivating and spreading love, we create a concrete activity, a describable finite, manageable set of behaviors, with many possible rewards and repercussions.

October 26

By focusing more on love, love grows. By addressing its functions, activities, and descriptions, we allow for many more positive feelings to expand, and infuse new life into them.

Thoughts can influence what ultimately transpires in life. Loving thoughts create an energy field of their own, an infinite source of renewal for the self and all nurturing relationships.

October 27

Evaluate your current level of the many expectations you have of yourself, and others, as a concrete task that relates to your specific program of change. If the levels of these expectations are too high, you may encounter continuous frustration without knowing exactly why. So, you may wish to reconsider or redefine your expectations, thus simplifying them. Even by relaxing a bit more, and going with the greater flow of interpersonal mindfulness, you can take great strides toward moving toward your deeper inner truths.

October 28

There are many who have helped us to see more clearly what our truly more pure spiritual nature of pathways or "greater flow" consists of compatible with our very short journeys here on earth. Most notably, our great spiritual leaders from many different cultures have done this for us. It has become easier to discuss these concepts as our common language of spirituality incorporates them, and this allows our consciousness in turn to continue to expand.

October 29

We are living our spirituality, in this sense, not only practicing it, on Sundays, or church days, or during Christmas, or Passover or any other religious holidays that emphasize love. We are then pursuing it in real, everyday life, not only within the confines of an organized religion's walls or in structured spiritual activities held at specific times.

October 30

Still craving and felt continually starved for more ways to integrate our spiritual development into our everyday lives we strive to share these deeper, ardently caring experiences even more, so we need to make them more of a clear priority in our lives. We need to bring ourselves closer and closer to each other and ourselves. We need to be prepared to emotionally suffer on deeper levels, in order to meet God, or the higher universe, or whatever, whoever we believe our maker to be.

October 31

And then, we will care more as a whole person, in a more holy manner, reflective of the other side. So, although we feel alone, we are not truly alone. We increasingly recognize that our energy is inextricably tied up with others and that most of what we do each day is connective in nature, and not individualized.

November 1

Take a moment and try to visualize your life on a typical kind of day, as a more loving being. This is another example of a concrete step. Upon reflecting on how this day would look to you, it may become much different from how it is now. What your requirements are in order that this happen? Does your day reflect the kind of holy encounters or service to others that you more deeply intended, or is it reflective of the higher level of loving interactions of your deeper self?

November 2

Is it possible to begin thinking more in this manner, each day, and to allow your spirituality to be more integrated into your daily dealings with others, as best as you possibly can? Are there other simple ways, along with daily readings such as these that you can use in order to nurture this side of yourself?

November 3

On this level, examine what really makes up your dealings with others. What do individuals in your daily life really mean to you? How much energy is put into your significant others, at work and in your family, on a regular basis? This element has to do with a sense of how to more authentically relate with other people.

November 4

Some higher forces have placed each of us on this earth, to be together, and intended, it seems, to make something significant with it for our learning, and beyond what any one of us can ever seem to know or imagine. We are taught many lessons through our relationships with others. Peaceful and loving coexistence on this planet is entirely possible, and many of us sense this. True intimacy with one another, as peaceful coexistence of one culture with another, is a totally attainable and highly feasible reality.

November 5

A renewed movement celebrating our loving humanness is possible. For many of us it is already occurring: It is no longer the stuff of outside fringe groups, but integrated right within the basic fabric of our society. If we begin to see the true inner beauty in the connecting, or in the sense of human dignity within our daily sacred interactions with others, more positive changes will occur. To really make a point of acknowledging this loving sanctity, no matter how small, how insignificant or brief, in a connection with others is essential, on a soul level.

November 6

All of our human interaction falls within this realm of spirit, a major building block of our whole interpersonal wellness process. Look more deeply now into the eyes of others around you. You can easily see that we each know of love, fear, pain and joy.

November 7

Sense the rhythms of the emotional spirit evident in all of your daily comings and goings with others. Watch your spirit move through others, as well as theirs through you. Observe this process, appreciate it, and love it. Experience your interactions with others as the spiritual, universal gifts that they are.

November 8

Gently dissolve away any useless defenses that you have, especially those that involve controlling others. They use interpersonal energy to no benefit and often cause additional stress. The deep self will have more room to positively shift and advance. This will indeed happen. By peeling away through useless defenses and moving toward a more interpersonally sacred connection with life, you will leave more room for your deeper loving essence to emerge. More doors will open as interpersonal wellness helps to move you toward a happier, healthier and fuller life of maximizing potential on all levels of being.

November 9

Many of us have emotionally blocked zones that consist of chronic emotional pain, boredom, guilt, rigid routines, and negatively self- destructive thoughts and behavior patterns. In order to break through them, we need to recognize that our thoughts, spirituality, and feelings, all need to work efficiently together.

November 10

We often would like to ask ourselves, how do we start this process, and achieve the point of breaking through our more blocked emotional zones? There is nothing magical or mystical about it. To shift our gears into this deeper place is kind of like changing from our usual emotional channels into a new way of being and thinking. It is a shift, ingrained into our everyday activities.

November 11

The human mind and heart are like giant satellite dishes for the spiritual energy all around us. There is plenty of this loving energy in our universe, and we only really need to learn how to harness it better. Love-focused living is like absorbing ever-present gamma waves-present everywhere in the universe. We only need to learn how to identify, access, and develop the energy.

November 12

It is a misconception that there is only so much love to go around, for it originates, or comes from a place way beyond our physical or phenomenological frame of reference, or, what our limited bodily senses are able to access. Like the collective unconscious, it occupies a place that is unknowable, yet we can feel certain of its existence. Love is a place of the spirit, a place of deep spirituality. It is a zone of being that pervades all that is.

November 13

Focus today and on each upcoming day in your life loving energy and its infinite force in the universe with boundless ramifications; utilize the loving energy with any combination of prayer, art, or meditation, in order to help yourself to gain more access to it.

November 14

Above all, utilize what you have learned thus far about a love-focused presence in your daily interactions with other people. Love is a limitless force. The proof of this is self-evident: Mindful loving is capable of helping one in achieving a joy of sacred interactions each and every day.

November 15

Often, the sharing and giving of love to others provides a most authentic and effective pathway to the inner self or psyche. Both love and joy share this purpose in our spirit life. Likely, one could not exist without the other.

November 16

We are each vastly different in expressions of body and soul, just as everything in this universe or in nature is different and uniquely created, from simple, organic life to the creation of snowflakes. Variation and creativity exist in many ways in an outer, external, and physical world as well as a world within us, both in seen and unseen patterns.

November 17

Any guide or plan, or combinations of plans that we choose for our self-improvement, should take this into account. This uniqueness, in order for it to be effective, must include the acknowledgment of love-focused energy. There are no easy blueprints that work for everybody. To begin with, take a simple, loving idea and breath it in, ever so slowly, deliberately, and mindfully, while visualizing your unique self or spirit surrounded by boundless love in this universe.

November 18

Recall any events in your life which have led you to this unique state of being today, right at this moment. Fantasize of some examples, especially of how this might mean putting your uniqueness to work in order to help improve the life around you in all of its forms.

November 19

Within this boundless space that we live in, and within the extremes of emotional nature and the reality of our daily existence, is the obvious, and clear, manifestation of love. Human relationships consist of the full range of possible emotions. Honest relationships, in particular, consist of sharing the full, intense ranges of compassion.

November 20

This is what is intended, or we would have been given a more limited range with which to work with in order to express our feelings, especially those dealing with love. Feelings, in their purest states, are forms of energy: psychic energy, like rays of light or heat, and as such, are meant to be expressed, meant to occupy their rightful places in this universe, along with the possible spectrums of other energy or events of nature.

November 21

As with other episodes in creation, the intent is not to be harmful or destructive, but to be lucid and fair. To try, while working at cultivating a more practiced existence of interpersonal mindfulness, to not to take everything that others may say personally, or self-centeredly is to realize that others need to express their range of feelings as well, and so they are on unique spiritual journeys as well.

November 22

Each of us is important, and we each may say something harmful while we do not intend to, or perhaps do not realize it. We need to give to one another, the benefit of the doubt more frequently. Do not automatically assume you are not well thought of; there are more positive thoughts out there about you than you would tend to think.

November 23

We cannot remember to say positive things all of the time, nor, to feel and share joy all of the time. Pain is a normal part of our human condition, because it is part of the necessary plan for our spiritual growth, and it is often connected to something far greater than us. Place things in this larger and more spiritual context, and the healing of self and relationships will begin to really nourish the psyche and be presented to you in a totally new way.

November 24

Just as the plant life that surrounds us grows through its various seasons, feelings must also have their cycles of nature, in order to exist and grow. The most action oriented form of loving and living that we can possibly have is derived from the source of the spirit, the most cherished and important part of us that fuels the many other portions of being. This growth process is given a huge boost when we start to view our life as a journey, a journey of learning, of self-improvement, and positive change. It becomes a journey filled with continual interpersonal wellness.

November 25

The central issue becomes, what do we want in this life, what is essential to give to others? What is deeply wished for? What needs to be different, right now in your life? What behaviors should be decreased increased, and how might you know when you are getting closer to your overall spiritual goal?

November 26

Life is more than it seems more than it appears to be at the surface levels. It is filled with emotional and moral undercurrents, every moment, no matter what the activity, and no matter how seemingly insignificant.

November 27

The energies of the unconscious, and the deep spiritual lessons and coincidences around us, are not coincidences after all. Upon closer examination, or with some distance of passing time, it becomes clear there is a loving, guiding, master plan.

November 28

These patterns that are so intricate, and evolved and involved, that, no one of us, nor any one particular group of us, will ever be able to fully see, recognize or control the whole process. This is the way of the spirit.

November 29

We should trust the process, learn our lessons, and move on.

The "process" of life can be so hard to see amidst our daily schedules, routine tasks and stressors. We often focus on what we do at the expense of how we do it; on what we do with others at the expense of how to be with them. Process is powerful, can be very loving and is embedded in all that we do.

November 30

List any three areas of desired change, with just one goal, relating to any combination of them. Check out your goal with one other person, either by sharing it or asking for some feedback. Realize that, as more is learned about the self, your plan can be continuously revised and your entire process continuously refined.

December 1

Realize how much more interpersonal wellness and the life processes of others begin to constitute the loving energy of your life. As you work harder and harder, and allow periods of rest, incubation, and down time, your growth still continues! This is because a process can continue within us, gently, even when we don't realize it, if we have put enough initial energy into it.

December 2

Staying still and keeping yourself focused on the total ability to relax, means, listening carefully to others, and relaxing your whole, entire body, spirit and mind. Try to keep your conscious mind focused on what a sense of well being, without any projections, or feelings of tension. Relaxation is something that can easily be learned.

December 3

It is a skill, much like driving or reading. The key is, most of us have not had the benefit of completely learning it. Relaxation's not instinctive to the human species. Yet it is becoming more and more imperative to learn it so that we can evoke and continue to more lovingly survive with less physically debilitating amounts of stress.

December 4

Make a conscious opportunity to relax, in any manner possible, by learning to breathe slowly, and deliberating focusing on something, listening well, or intently doing something, and take brief rest periods so that significant gains can be made in this area.

December 5

Learning relaxation skills is still largely a manner of learning how to attain small skills and then building upon them. Most of the skills involve slowing down, acknowledging love, mindfully relating to others, relearning new behaviors, and having new thoughts of how to have enlivened feelings, without having the tensions or negative projections or thoughts.

December 6

While working on this, we learn to look at overall communication styles, particularly with those in close relationships, on any given day.

Ask yourself if there is much questioning you have of how others live their lives. Are there too many demands that you place upon others? Is there too little active listening of their concerns? Is there good eye contact between you and others? Interruptions? What occurs if someone brings up a risky or scary topic to you? Is there a lot of tension, a lot of compressed affect? Is there a lot of the external clutter or chatter, such as gossip, or talk about the weather, the latest films, and politics?

December 7

How is your communication time used in your interpersonal life? Everyone around you, including yourself, is a potential helper, healer, minister, and teacher. If there is not a close network of trusting, and loving, friends, or trusting relationships around you, then, there needs to be work done on developing one.

December 8

A simple place is needed where there is safety enough to express oneself directly. Directness often causes more good than harm in this world, and if we are more loving about it and it feels safe, it can be enormously healing. Perhaps when all is said and done, it will have been our inner worlds that will have needed the most exploring and will have mattered the most.

December 9

We each possess a vast, mysterious and wondrous creation within our very beings. Yet our inner beings are not easy grounds for exploration. We do not easily visualize the inner self as a place to journey. We have little trouble imagining a journey into outer space or to another country, or even into the nearby woods. But the excursion within requires far less energy, disruption, fuel, or preparation and is, at times, far more inviting than the obvious external excitement of a physical trip.

December 10

Our inner world is always accessible, always prepared for our visitations, and most of the time, welcomes us. The choice of our types of journeys is a profoundly personal one. What each journey offers us is one of the great paradoxes of life: Most can be gained by even the most simple and obvious of steps, and most can be procured when we stop fighting the process, and give in to our divine nature.

December 11

Take two trips today. One inside of yourself, and one outside of yourself. Here's how: Take a short walk, or, go outdoors for a brief period of time, perhaps for just five minutes. Look all around you. Journey with your senses into this "outside world." Notice and take in everything. Next, at another time period of this day, meditate for five minutes. Just sit calmly, close your eyes, and listen to what thoughts are there within you. Pay close and loving attention to any inner images, memories, sounds. Think of love.

December 12

This emotionally prosperous journey never ends. Smugness and complacency about the deepest personal and innermost growth are to be avoided, because they can do much damage. No one ever truly arrives at full self actualization. Fully arriving is not the way that changes, or that any kind of loving change works in the ways of the world. This is the way of the ego. Watch out for placing others on pedestals, for they will no doubt eventually fall off.

December 13

The best teacher lives within you. Others, such as parents, teachers, ministers, priests, coaches, can also hold up the light. They cannot walk your path for you, ever.

Our work is unique, and likely will be, into eternity. Our human ego, or egocentric way of life, ultimately requires a change, or an asking for help. Be cautious and careful, and gentle with the help for your spirit. The ego has not as much power as it thinks it has been given. Authentic interpersonal wellness is often interfered with by the falsities of the ego.

December 14

We are traveling, all taking this journey together. Individually, we travel, yet we travel as a group. Being fully human is being willing to travel yet not to a specific geographical place. The geography outside of us is pretty, and it can be unbelievably healing, yet it is not the true place of the soul, of our inner soul. To travel within means a willingness to move and trust that our spiritual ride is a loving one, loaded with renewal, pain, surprises and guides.

December 15

Growth comes, sometimes, at those times it is least expected. Go to some unusual feeling places today. Go easy, and if too uneasy, try another time. Go into a group. Try something that is open, free, and welcoming. It does no harm to try. Your higher self is not really a judge. It does not issue orders or put you down. Instead, your higher self loves you in a detached way. It helps you to learn from your mistakes, to seek your inner bliss, and not to judge others as well.

December 16

The higher self knows it is an integral part of this whole earth, just as its rivers, mountains, trees and streams, and it seeks the love-focused way. It can remove any self-defeating, self-constructed prisons of your mind when you fully trust it to do so. So be gentle with it, allow it to do its work, and be sensitively guided along.

December 17

The higher self hears the sounds of the flowers and learns the earth's seasons and pushes you ever so gently toward the light. Notice the light in all of your interactions. Take note of how many things are affected by it, move toward it, or away from it, as it travels gently into our lives during the day. Who controls this light? Its love-focused powers, through our caring mindfulness of others, help us to connect to the power of this light.

December 18

Interpersonal wellness works with the deepest sense of gratitude. Feeling a sense of gratitude for all that has been given to us in this life, is a door that swings open, into a large room filled with exquisite emotion, and the potential for a more love focused, energized life. Through gratitude we can feel renewed energy, and by walking through this door, we can allow the experience of interpersonal light to occur and invite others to share in it with us. This room is filled with spiritual tools, and once there, one never wants to leave. For life outside of this kind of "connected light" way of being never looks the same way to us again.

December 19

Love-focused behaviors easily can become a natural way of life. In all of our actions, every day, we can rest assured that increasingly mindful energy moves outward from us, into the universe, and into other places, as if to activate more resources. It is put to more loving and healing purposes. It is, like any other energy or force of this universe, never destroyed, and always conserved for life-giving and life sustaining purposes. It changes form, moves forward, and goes elsewhere to do its work. Such is the way of something as simple as gratitude.

December 20

Look all around you. Realize what is out there and freely given in this gift of loving. Interpersonal mindfulness with others works in just this way in all of your daily encounters.

Life is about loss and meaning. Death is part of nature, and grief is a part of life. Yet to recognize grief is to recognize love. And in order to fully live and grow emotionally, we need to go through a death of sorts, our psyche's ego. We need to let go of who we thought we might be, and more fully accept who we are; who we have become as a part of all of our experiences in life and we soon realize that this period of mourning and grieving is also a period of re-birthing of re-parenting, with the deepest self of the spirit as our chief nurturer. It is at once how we learn to connect without ego, and see that we cannot get this kind of pure nurturing from anyone or anything else but spirit.

December 21

The past can never be changed nor ever be fully healed, yet with the gift of the present we begin to proactively and emotionally regenerate and engage in a happier, more joyful life.

Along your way, sharing with others and creating pathways of interpersonal mindfulness ultimately transforms reality. At the end, it is one's own individual, unique, pattern of joy and pain that teaches. There is no individual soul in this universe that feels exactly the same as another at any given point in time. No one's pattern of attaining interpersonal wellness is the same, nor, is their pattern of overall healing. At times, we may feel "down," or have the need to think, be alone, or be in solitude yet not in loneliness. Remember that you are never alone with the spirit. Spirit connects each of us, one to the other.

December 22

So instead of mustering up the energy to be powerful, or perfect, in order to satisfy others, begin to take the risks of interpersonal wellness reflected upon here and ever so slowly, be known more authentically, including to yourself. Gently connect with others. Slowly reveal your imperfect, inconsistent, good, bad, weak, strong and all too human, loving self to this world in the most loving way imaginable. Happiness becomes the journey of building together in relation, with interpersonal mindfulness serving as the glue for a world of interpersonal wellness. Live peacefully and mindfully and all aspects of love will flow towards you and within you.

December 23

Life is in many ways about the experience of vibration. Matter and energy are comprised of vibration just as are consciousness and feelings.

The beauty of all that we see is that is in constant motion, constant change, and constant vibration.

December 24

There is in the vibratory world of feelings, identifiable healthy and loving levels of feelings as well as painful, dark, toxic levels. We often struggle and wonder if we have any control over their existence or influence upon us.

December 25

The holiday season illustrates quite powerfully how the energy level around us is changed as people raise their level of feeling vibration to a more loving and compassionate level. How is this done? Who is in charge? What better choices can we make for ourselves this season and always?

December 26

Holiday imagery is consistently positive, filled with images of loving beings, angels, guides, representatives of God, holy words, sacred ceremonies. Is it no wonder that the vibratory level of energy is raised beyond its normal levels?

This is also the case at times of death, extreme grief or loss or events that are defined by a spiritual context.

December 27

How can we create a higher level of vibratory energy on a feeling level so that we can achieve a higher level of potential on the cognitive and spiritual levels as well?

One exercise to visualize is the feeling around the heart or chest area, that energy that often connects to others on a feeling level, and consciously tries to, with the mind, imagine a higher or more pure level of vibration.

December 28

Begin with loving and positive thoughts as well, visualizing a sacred connection, unseen, from your mind area to the others. Such a connection is with us and has as its source something greater also, which will thus energize the connection even more.

December 29

This exercise or way of being is thinking with the heart a process that is very different from our normal mind or body orientation. Spiritually, in prayer we visualize our connection to God, Jesus, Buddha or Allah, and so on, yet in relation, from one living being to the other, we do not routinely think with our heart unless the context warrants it, such as holy holiday or funeral.

December 30

Begin to lay the foundation for the coming year. Concentrate on thinking with the heart. As the focus or foundation of your thoughts you will be surprised at the level of energy created in your other typical thinking realms as well.

December 31

Always pray. Stay in conscious contact with the being greater than yourself and many surprises and unexpected levels of guidance will enter your life. There is more room to connect here, as well as with those whom you love who have departed the physical realm, than you would expect.

Suggestions for Further Reading

Abbott, E.A.(1952) <u>Flatland</u>. Dover Publications.

Buber, M.(1970) <u>I and Thou</u>. Charles Scribner's Sons: NY.

Davies, P.(1992) <u>The Mind of God</u>: <u>The Scientific Basis for a Rational World</u>.Touchstone: NY.

Ferguson, M.(1987) <u>The Aquarian Conspiracy</u>: <u>Personal and Social Transformation in our Time</u>. Tarcher/St. Martin's Press: NY.

Frankl, V.E.(1984) <u>Man's Search for Meaning</u> Touchstone: NY.

Kierkegaard, S.(1995) <u>Works of Love</u>. Princeton University Press.

Peat, F.D.(1987) <u>Synchronicity: The Bridge Between Matter and Mind</u>. Bantam Books: NY.

Prakash, P.(1998) <u>The Yoga of Spiritual Devotion Inner Traditions</u>: Rochester, VT.

Rechtschaffen, S. (1996) <u>Time shifting: Creating More Time to Enjoy Your Life</u>. Doubleday: NY.

Ridley, B.K.(1994) <u>Time, Space and Things</u>. Cambridge University Press.
Rogers, C.(1961) <u>On Becoming A Person</u>. Houghton Mifflin: Boston, MA.

Sheldrake, R.(1995) <u>Seven Experiments That Could Change the World</u>. Riverhead Books: NY

Wilheim, R. (1979) <u>Lectures on the I Ching: Constancy and Change</u>. Princeton University Press.

Zukav, G.(1980) <u>The Dancing Wu Li Masters</u>. Bantam Books: N